ILLUMINATED MANUSCRIPTS IN HUNGARY

ILLUMINATED MANUSCRIPTS IN HUNGARY

XI-XVI CENTURIES

by

ILONA BERKOVITS

translated by

ZSUZSANNA HORN

revised by

ALICK WEST

FREDERICK A. PRAEGER, *Publishers*

New York · Washington

BOOKS THAT MATTER

Published in the United States of America in 1969
by Frederick A. Praeger, Inc., Publishers
111 Fourth Avenue, New York, N.Y. 10003

Library of Congress Catalog Card Number: 69-11964

Printed in Hungary

116270

CONTENTS

MINIATURE PAINTING IN HUNGARY

No other people of Central Europe has suffered such tragic losses of its ancient cultural treasures as have the Hungarians. The number of Hungarian volumes of the Middle Ages destroyed by the wars that ravaged the country cannot be estimated. Besides this destruction of manuscripts, numerous profusely adorned illuminated codices have found their way to other countries, and now enrich the collections of the most important libraries of the world. Nearly three-quarters of the surviving manuscripts from the famous library of Matthias Corvinus, the great Hungarian Renaissance sovereign, in addition to several documents of Romanesque and Gothic miniature painting, are to be found in collections outside Hungary.

The whole of Hungarian miniature painting cannot be adequately treated in the present work. Through the description of outstanding works preserved in Hungary—and also of some important volumes in other countries—it is intended to give a general survey of Hungarian medieval miniature painting from its beginnings at the close of the 10th century, to the end of the 16th century, when as a result of the spread of printing the writing and illuminating of manuscripts no longer answered any need and gradually ceased.

OSZK = Országos Széchényi Könyvtár (National Széchényi Library), Budapest
EK = Egyetemi Könyvtár (University Library), Budapest
FK = Főszékesegyházi Könyvtár (Cathedral Library), Esztergom

THE BEGINNINGS OF MINIATURE PAINTING

In Hungary the beginnings of miniature painting coincided with the introduction of Christianity.

At the close of the 10th century and at the opening of the 11th, when the Hungarians were converted to Christianity and became part of the western religious and cultural community, the illumination of manuscripts in Europe could look back upon a brilliant past. After the downfall of the Western Empire (476) the writing of manuscripts and miniature painting were continued or reborn at two extreme points of the world as it was then known. From Byzantium and Ireland the book started on its career of world conquest and became the foundation and the bearer of medieval civilization. Byzantine culture bears witness to an advanced miniature art, which under the guidance of monumental art was to exert a fruitful influence on European art. During the upheaval of the Migrations, the cultivation of manuscript writing and of the new art was not only practised in Byzantium; it also began in Ireland, thanks to her favourable geographical position, and spread thence to the European continent. As primitive man had decorated the walls of caves or the conquering Hungarians coming from Asia had decorated the saddles and harnesses of their horses, so the monks of Irish monasteries decorated letters. Between the written lines they gave free play to their imagination, and enlivened the large initial capital letter with stylized figures of animals and interlacings with intricate patterns. Human figures also began to appear in a stylized form; like the figures of animals, they were employed particularly as decorative motifs. Often letters themselves were fashioned of animals, of motifs derived from fishes, serpents and birds. This was new and strange, almost barbaric, alien to the art of ancient civilizations. The motifs were borrowed from goldsmiths' designs, and partitioned ornamentation was applied to adorn parchment. These decorative motifs, enriched with oriental elements, later came into general use all over Europe.

In the second half of the 8th century Charlemagne, the monarch of the new Western Empire, showed understanding, not only in politics, but also in learning, for the spirit of the time. At his court and in his empire copyists' workshops and painters' studios were established, and here Carolingian miniature painting was born. At this time early medieval painting had progressed no further than miniature painting. In the compositions embodying several figures there was drama and inner fire. The striving for decorative effect was inspired with restless ardour, and in the late Carolingian age the delicate tracery of line became ever more animated. Inner tension disrupted contours and created such forms as usually characterize the highest periods of artistic achievement. In the 10th century, when independent states had emerged—the Italian, French and German empires—Carolingian miniature art was already declining. European miniature painting was enriched with new, Byzantine elements partly by the intermediary of Italian art. Thus at the close of the 10th century the styles earlier cultivated in Ireland and Byzantium at the extreme points of Europe, had almost merged. German miniature painting had reached a great height in post-Carolingian times, but it never gained such general acceptance in Europe as had Carolingian miniature art. It was in the 10th century that individual styles of miniature art became distinguishable in the various monastery schools, though they all continued to draw on their common source in Carolingian miniature art which still made itself felt in the 11th century, when the Hungarians, having embraced Christianity, became part of Western European civilization.

The miniature was of great importance in ancient Hungarian art. In many cases it conveyed and reflected the ideas of the age with more intensity than did any other form of art. Closely related to other products of contemporary Hungarian art, the illumination of manuscripts was generally in advance of them, and often exerted an influence on monumental art. Early Hungarian panel painting was inspired by miniatures, and though they would seem the most contrary art to mural painting, miniatures are even echoed in frescoes.

From the early centuries of Hungarian art very few illuminated manuscripts with miniatures have come down to us. In the wars and fires of subsequent centuries, in the Mongol invasion (1241–42), the disastrous battle of Mohács (1526), and in the long Turkish rule that was to follow, most of the old volumes were destroyed. It is to be supposed that a great number of illuminated manuscripts from Hungary are lying unidentified in the libraries of other countries.

After his coronation as king of Hungary (in 1000), (St) Stephen I (997–1038) speedily proceeded to organize the Church; besides building fortresses to strengthen defence, he established bishoprics and monasteries in quick succession. King Stephen's foreign relations extended to every part of Europe. From Byzantium, Monte Cassino, Rome, Venice, Dalmatia, Cluny, Chartres, St Gallen, Fulda and Regensburg there flowed into Hungary ideas which welded Hungarians into one great community; thus there was brought into being—where necessary by force—a new, progressive Hungarian Christian civilization, rich in potentiality. The foundation of churches and monasteries necessitated the production of ecclesiastical ritual books; and both the building of churches and the production of ritual books were not only notable stages in the history of liturgy and religion, but also of decisive importance for the development of Hungarian art. King Stephen's patronage of art and letters actually marked the beginning of Hungarian art. Stone-masons and master builders arrived from Byzantium and Italy, and in erecting the first cathedrals they laid the foundations of Hungarian Romanesque architecture. At the same time, the leading Hungarian statesmen were in close touch with prominent personalities of the western world. Stephen I carried on a correspondence with St Odilo, the celebrated Abbot of Cluny. The first Bishop of Pécs, the Frenchman Bonipert, sent a request for books to Fulbert de Chartres. This period witnessed also the first literary activities. St Gerard (Gellért), a Venetian, retired for two years to the seclusion of a forest hut at Bakonybél to write books, one of which, entitled *Deliberationes* (Meditations), has survived. An unknown monk—perhaps of Pannonhalma—wrote chronicles in which he recorded for posterity the ecclesiastical and secular events of his age. A court chaplain of Stephen I wrote a work with the title *De institutione morum* (Exhortations).

When the Hungarians first became Christians, their books undoubtedly came from other countries, but they soon began to copy the texts and to imitate the decorations. Although books were valued as rare and costly treasures and writing was considered a difficult craft, by the end of the century, in 1093, there were as many as 80 illuminated manuscripts at Pannonhalma—an astonishingly large number when we recall that at the beginning of the 9th century Würzburg, founded in the 8th century, possessed only 36 books, while Cologne had 100 codices. Other interesting figures may be given: at the close of the 13th century there were 122 illuminated manuscripts at Klosterneuburg; the Abbey of Bakonybél owned 84 manuscript volumes before the Mongol invasion (1241–42).

Nevertheless, not a single illuminated manuscript of Stephen I's age has survived, although there is proof of the king having made donations of books to churches. At his court charters were written, and it may be presumed that books also were copied. Indeed, there is also evidence that as early as the 11th century books were taken from Hungary to other countries. An illuminated manuscript belonging to St Elizabeth of Hungary, the *Psalterium Gertrudis*—a magnificent work of Trier from the late 10th century, now at Cividale—was taken to Russia in the 11th century by the Hungarian princess Gertrud, who became the consort of a Russian prince. From the Hungarian literature of the period of Stephen I nothing survives except in later copies. Thus the Chronicles (997–1060) have come down to us in the Pray Manuscript of the 12th century; the only surviving work of Bishop Gerard, the *Deliberationes*, may be found as a plain, unadorned copy from the 11th century in the State Library of Munich. *De institutione morum* and the laws of St Stephen have been preserved in copies from later periods.

In the last quarter of the 11th century, during the reign of (St) Ladislas I (1077–1095), feudal culture came to full development in Hungary. The first literary work was written on Hungarian soil in the 1060s: St Maurice, Bishop of Pécs, wrote an account of the martyrdom of Zoerard and Benedict, the hermits of Zoborhegy (now Zobor, Czechoslovakia). Legends about the doings of the first Hungarian king, his son, Prince Emeric, and the martyred bishop, Gerard, handed on by word of mouth, were a living memory among the people. By order of Ladislas I the legend of St Stephen was committed to writing; this was the first chronicle of Hungarian history.

The oldest manuscript written in Hungary has come down to posterity from the second half of the 11th century: the Sacramentary of Hahót (Zagreb, Archiepiscopal Library, MR 126) was produced between 1060 and 1080, certainly before 1083. This was followed by the volume known as the Szelepchényi Evangelistary (Nitra, Capitular Archives 118) which, according to the most recent literature on Hungarian liturgy, was written at the close of the 11th century—perhaps in the early 12th century—for the monastery of Garamszentbenedek (now Hronský Beňadik, Czechoslovakia).

Although in its details the illumination of the Hahót and Szelepchényi Manuscripts conforms to the accepted style of 11th-century European miniature painting, yet in general character it reveals a difference. For there was not, nor could there be, any artistic tradition which continued the glowing intensity and the nervous restlessness of capricious line characteristic of Carolingian work.

The Hungarians could acquire Carolingian culture only from its aftermath in the foreign trends reaching the country in the 11th century.

But although the motifs in Hungarian miniature painting did not spring from the native soil but had been created by the general artistic culture of Christianity, it is not impossible that the strivings of early Hungarian miniature painting towards simplification were inspired by the balanced, calm style which at the time of the Magyar Conquest the goldsmiths cultivated in their art. This assumption is supported particularly by the calligraphy of some letters to be seen in the manuscript of Hahót, even though in some ornamental motifs the influence of Byzantium, Monte Cassino and Dalmatia is clearly discernible. The Szelepchényi Manuscript is more richly illuminated than the Sacramentary of Hahót. The eminent master of the former began his text by painting a decoration which covered nearly half of the sheet, and he gave special importance to the opening word; the letters themselves with their decorative forms sumptuously adorned the page.

In the Szelepchényi Evangelistary the type of the initials is uniform throughout. The miniaturist avoided the looping of scrolls and connected them with bands instead. This peculiar feature was to persist also in the 12th century (Fig. 1). The master of the Hahót Manuscript, on the other hand, shows greater variety in the use of initials; he employs various decorative motifs, both figures and scroll, including a very small and simple representation of a man's head. There is also striking variety in the colouring of letters. In this manuscript are to be seen letters with scroll ornament, coloured with the bronzed green paint which had come into vogue in the workshops of numerous European miniaturists, indicating Byzantine and Dalmatian influence. Similar letters may be found in 12th-century Hungarian miniature art, for instance in the monumental Csatár Bible, and in the manuscript of Bernard of Perugia.

The illumination of both the Sacramentary of Hahót and the Szelepchényi Evangelistary is in complete harmony with 11th-century Hungarian Romanesque art. Motifs employed in the designs of initials may also be found in the ornamentation of fragments of cornices, capitals and columns from churches.

In the 12th century Hungarian Romanesque art made notable progress. New churches were built, while older cathedrals were enriched with monumental works of extraordinary beauty, and with sculptures and mural paintings which later suffered destruction. Literary education also advanced. As early as in the reign of Könyves Kálmán (Coloman Beauclerc; 1095–1116) liturgical plays and dramatized scenes from the Bible were performed. Yet not a single book owned by this highly educated monarch has come down to posterity. Indeed, of all the manuscripts written, illuminated and adorned in 12th-century Hungary fewer than ten have survived, most of them plainly executed.

Of the simply decorated manuscripts produced in Hungary in the 12th century, the first to be mentioned is the Antiphonary of Graz, referred to as *Codex Albensis* (Graz, University Library), prepared at Székesfehérvár in the first half of the century. The rather plain initial *A*, painted in two colours, red and black, is closely related to the simpler initials of the Hahót Sacramentary, where also only two colours are used. The initial word of the text, the letters of which are further accentuated by being written in majuscules, also displays characteristic features of the Hahót Sacramentary. The style of the pen drawings to be found on four pages of this volume is less easy to define. They show a curious variation in the number of ornamental elements typical of earlier and later epochs, and it remains doubtful whether they are of the 12th century.

The so-called Ernst Manuscript (Budapest, OSZK Clmae 431), which contains the oldest copy of the legend of St Stephen and a version of the life of St Martin, was also produced in the 12th century. Its delicate initials derive directly from the initials in the Hahót and Szelepchényi Manuscripts. The unpretentious initials painted in minium in the manuscript known as the Admont Manuscript (Budapest, OSZK Clmae 433) deserve to be regarded as works of art. Decorated with bands and foliated design, the letters follow the decorative style of the initials to be seen in the Szelepchényi, Hahót and Ernst Manuscripts. The volume *Haymonis episcopi Homiliae* now in Rumania (Alba Iulia [Gyulafehérvár], Batthyanaeum), which belonged to the Dominicans of Kassa (now Košice, Czechoslovakia) in the 13th century, is also to be grouped with these works of art, and likewise a fragment of six pages from a lectionary (Sopron, Municipal Archives No. 154).

Besides these manuscripts of modest execution there is a monumental work of art in two bulky volumes, namely the lavishly decorated manuscript which used to be at Admont (Austria) and has passed into the possession of the National Library of Vienna, known as the Gutkeled, or Admont, or Csatár Bible (Vienna, National

5

uobis. quia non nouerunt patrem neq; me. Sed hec locutus sum uobis. ut cum uenerit hora eorum reminiscamini quia ego dixi uobis. IN VIGLA PENTECOSTEN. SEC. IOHEM.

In illo tempore. Dixit ihc discipulis suis. Si diligitis me mandata mea seruate. Et ego rogabo patrem et alium paraclitum dabit uobis ut maneat uobiscum in eternum. spm ueritatis quem mundus non potest accipere. quia non uidet eum nec scit eum. Vos autem cognoscetis eum. quia apud uos manebit et in uobis erit. Non uos relinquam orphanos. uenIam ad uos. Adhuc modicum. et mundus me iam non uidet. Vos autem uidetis me. quia ego uiuo et uos uiuetis. In illo die uos cognoscetis quia ego in patre meo. et uos in me. et ego in uobis. Qui habet mandata mea et seruat ea. ille est qui diligit me. Qui autem diligit me. diligetur a patre meo. Et ego diligam eum. et manifestabo me ipsum. IN DIE SCO. SECVNDVM IOHEM.

In illo tempore. Dixit ihesus discipulis suis. Si quis diligit me. sermonem meum seruabit. Et pater meus diliget eum. et ad eum ueniemus. et mansionem apud eum faciemus. Qui non diligit me. sermones meos non seruat. Et sermonem quem audistis non est meus. sed eius qui misit me patris. Hec locutus sum uobis. apud uos manens. Paraclitus autem sps scs quem mittet pater in nomine meo. ille uos docebit omnia et suggeret uobis omnia quecumq; dixero uobis. Pacem relinquo uobis. pacem meam do uobis. Non quomodo mundus dat. ego do uobis. Non turbetur cor urm. neq; formidet. Audistis quia ego dixi uobis. uado et uenio ad uos. Si diligeretis me gauderetis utiq; quia uado ad patrem. quia pater maior me est. Et nunc dixi uobis priusquam fiat. ut cum factum

Library, Cod. Ser. n. 2701–2702). In older Austrian literature this work was mentioned also as the Gebhardt Bible and regarded as a manuscript produced in Salzburg. It was the property of the Benedictine monastery of Csatár in Zala County, founded in 1138; later, in the 13th century, it was pawned by the patron of the Abbey of Csatár, Wyd of the Gutkeled clan. How highly this Bible was valued is shown by the fact that in compensation for having pawned the two volumes the patron in 1263 made a gift to the Abbey of Csatár of two villages and two profitable estates, one by the river Mura, the other in Somogy County. A century later the Bible was already at Admont.

The high standard of Hungarian Romanesque art justifies the assumption that miniature painting must have been of a similarly high quality, though we possess few illuminated manuscripts from the period. Despite this lack, other outstanding works of contemporary Hungarian art prove convincingly that the Csatár Bible is a flowering of Hungarian art. To have shown its relation to Hungarian Romanesque miniature painting is the merit in the first place of Tibor Gerevich. The Bible is decorated with extraordinary profusion, and the miniatures are deeply imbued with the spirit of contemporary Hungarian art. In their style they are often related to other Hungarian works of art, particularly to frescoes surviving from the 11th and 12th centuries, as those in the church of Feldebrő. We also find similar artistic strivings in 12th-century sculpture, for instance at Pécs, in reliefs by the artist known as the Master of the Samson Scenes (1140–1150), and in those of the Master of the Nativity.

In addition to their splendid miniatures, the two volumes of the Csatár Bible are adorned with bronzed green foliated scroll, also with elaborate initials decorated with dragon motifs, as well as with plainer initials of calligraphic character decorated with bands, which are of kindred quality with the characteristic letter types of 11th and 12th-century Hungarian illuminated manuscripts. A miniature at the beginning of the Bible (Vol. I, fol. 3v) which covers the whole page and represents six scenes from Genesis is unfortunately badly damaged. The worn parts, however, clearly illustrate the origin of the word miniature: for we can see how on the thick parchment this outstanding artist first sketched his magnificent miniature in minium paint. The artist follows Byzantine and Carolingian traditions, and he is also affected by influences from France, St Gallen and Regensburg, but the individuality of his style is extremely interesting. Motifs from nature—rocks and flowers—are painted in gay colours and forms of a Baroque fantasy quite remote from reality. They contrast strongly with the faithful representation of human figures and with the astonishingly realistic painting of birds, and particularly of clumsy brown bears. Among the impressive miniatures in the exceedingly lavish illumination of the first volume the illustration of the Book of Ruth (fol. 107v) is of great interest, since it is the first representation in Hungarian art of harvesting. With a rhythmic, even movement three servants are reaping with their sickles in the field of Boaz, while Ruth, following in their footsteps, bends down to glean the ears of barley left by the reapers.

2

The Csatár Bible is not in Hungary. There are, however, in the country two illuminated manuscripts whose painted decorations are related to the same school. The volume in Esztergom bearing the title *Expositiones in Cantica Canticorum* (Esztergom, FK Ms. II. 3) was prepared in the style of the initials in the Csatár Bible, with bronzed and green foliated design and dragon motifs, as was also the manuscript known as the Pray Manuscript (Budapest, OSZK MNY 1), containing the earliest work of any length written in the Hungarian language, the Funeral Oration. The manuscript *Expositiones in Cantica Canticorum* was donated by Bernard of Perugia (who died in 1217), the Italian tutor of King Béla III's son, Prince Emeric, the later Archbishop of Spalato, to the St Adalbert Cathedral in Esztergom, after the fire of 1196, but the illumination of this manuscript may have been executed much earlier than the date of its presentation. It is one of those works of average quality of which, it may be presumed, a considerable number were at that time produced in Hungary (Fig. 2).

The Pray Manuscript was prepared at Boldva in the ancient Benedictine monastery. Its date is considered to be the end of the 12th century, between 1192 and 1195, but the style of its miniatures shows resemblance to the art associated with the middle of the century. It is not impossible that the miniaturist followed the illumination of an earlier, more elaborate manuscript, from the end of the 11th or the beginning of the 12th century, which has since been lost, and copied its compositions. On four pages of this volume, after the *Micrologus* and before the Calendar, there are large pen-and-ink drawings. Two of them cover a whole page, Christ on the Cross (fol. 27; Plate I) and the Deposition (fol. 27v; Plate II). On the next page the illuminator has depicted two scenes, such as may also be seen in some miniatures of the Csatár Bible, one, the Entombment, above, the other, the Visit to the Sepulchre, below (fol. 28; Plate III). Finally, on the upper part of the page is represented Christ Enthroned with the Angel Holding the Instruments of Torture (fol. 28v; Plate IV). Contrary to the splendour of the Csatár Bible, here the miniaturist seems not even to have had paints of different colour. His monumental compositions are in the colours of calligraphy, minium and blue, which creates a bizarre impression. The drawings are simple, but in their masterly composition they follow the style of the Csatár Bible and show close stylistic relationship to the reliefs of Pécs mentioned above; their affinity to some figures of the sculptor of Pécs known as the Master of the Nativity becomes evident at the first glance.

At this time liturgical books were illuminated also elsewhere in Hungary in a style similar to that of the decorations in the Pray Manuscript. The valuable Missal from the library of the Franciscan order of Németújvár (now Güssing, Austria) with its Canon coloured in minium and yellow is an example.

This concludes our account of illuminated manuscripts known from the 11th and 12th centuries. We now turn to material from the 13th century.

Until quite recently only one outstanding work of Hungarian origin was known, namely the *Gesta* of Anonymus (Budapest, OSZK Clmae 403). It is, however, unlikely that this century should have passed without any contribution being made to the history of Hungarian miniature painting, or that nothing noteworthy was produced by Hungarian miniaturists. We know nothing about the number of books destroyed in Hungary at the time of the Mongol invasion. There are records of illuminated manuscripts being lost through fire and pillage. For example, the fires at Veszprém and Székesfehérvár in the 13th century destroyed the libraries of the cathedrals of both these towns. We know from surviving evidence that there were book-lovers among the Hungarian aristocracy of the 12th century. Before setting out, in 1153, on a journey to Roger II, King of Sicily, Adalbert, ambassador of Hungarian King Géza II, made a will by which in the event of his death during his mission he bequeathed to the Benedictine monastery of Pannonhalma all his estates and books.

At the close of the 12th century, Hungarian intellectual life was stimulated and quickened under the reign of Béla III (1173–1196). In his youth the King had been educated at Byzantium as the heir to the throne of the Emperor Manuel. He married twice, and since both his consorts came from France, the French culture of his court exerted a decisive influence on 13th-century Hungarian civilization. Though no illuminated manuscripts of Hungarian origin are known from the age of Béla III, documents have survived. At the end of the 12th century and in the 13th century Hungarian charters were highly elaborate; they began with a large initial, and the first word, usually the king's name, was given special importance by being written in ornate calligraphic letters. Later, human figures and shapes of animals were also concealed among the calligraphic flourishes of the letters. In the 13th century Hungarian royal charters followed the style of French documents.

In the 13th century a similarity can be observed between chancellery charters and the illuminated manuscripts of monasteries. Most probably the manuscript containing the *Gesta* of Anonymus was copied at the monastery of some order in the second half of the 13th century. The original of the *Gesta* was most likely produced about the turn of the 12th century. The title-page was illuminated in the style employed by the royal chancellery to decorate documents; the plain initial *P* painted in two colours, in scarlet and green, was executed in the French style cultivated by the chancellery for the adornment of its charters (Fig. 3).

A cartulary, the *Libellus Ruber*, was prepared at Pannonhalma before 1240. Its small initials also follow the French calligraphic style of the chancellery, though the execution is more modest. Presumably in the 13th century not only the writing of royal charters may have resembled artistically that of French documents, but also the more elaborate illumination of manuscripts may have been executed in a style similar to that of French and secular miniaturists. Study of the decorations in some of our 14th-century illuminated manuscripts justifies the assumption of earlier French influence; indeed a continuous succession of Hungarian students received their education in France, and at the close of the century Alexander de Hungaria from the Augustine order became professor of the Sorbonne in Paris.

Recent research has identified an exceedingly valuable manuscript executed in Hungary—most probably in the second half of the 13th century—the volume *Concordantia Discordantium Canonum* (Bratislava, Capitular Library No. 14). The smaller miniatures with figures and the initials on six pages of this manuscript prove, without the need of any written evidence or of any theory, that in the age of the House of Árpád the production of books had reached an extraordinarily high cultural level, and that it was strongly influenced by France. The figures and the faces in these miniatures show an amazing likeness to

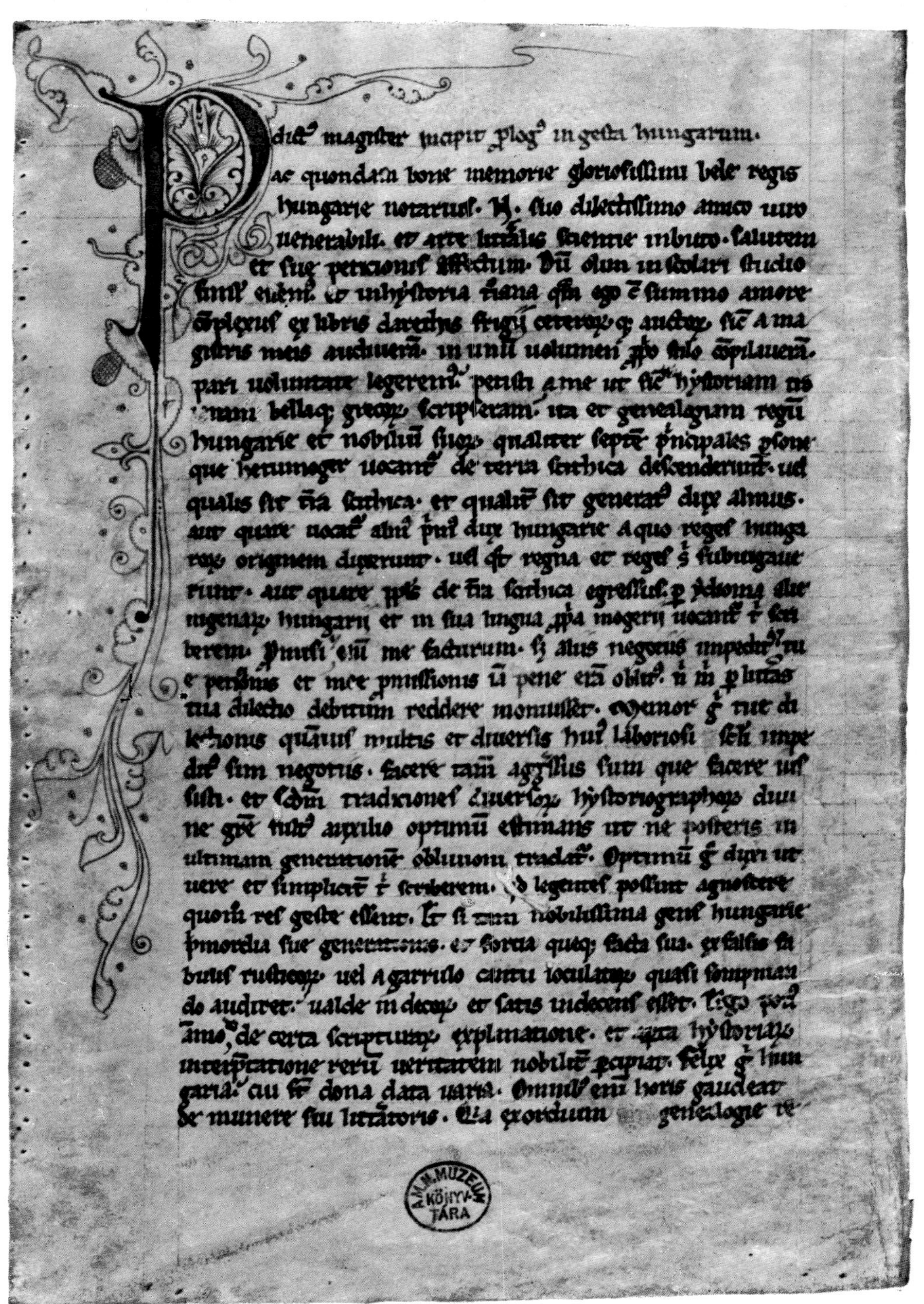

3

the fragment of an elbow-rest inlaid with marble from an archiepiscopal throne in the museum of stonework remains of Esztergom. Tibor Gerevich has dated this fragment to the second half of the 12th century, stressing that its ornamental motifs recall the miniatures of illuminated manuscripts, and the artist must have derived these motifs from book illumination.

Towards the end of the reign of the House of Árpád (13th century) Hungarian culture began to show signs of the Italian influences which were to assert themselves in a mature form in the art of the Anjou period. Relations with Italy, which had been maintained since the reign of Stephen I, gradually became closer, and in the second half of this century, from 1263, numerous Hungarian names are encountered in cartularies in the archives of the University of Bologna. The last Hungarian king from the House of Árpád, Andrew III (1290–1301), had an Italian mother and he was educated at Venice. During the ten years of his reign the intellectual life of the court still moved within the earlier tradition, but in courtly education there were already signs of that brilliance which was to acquire an Italian character under the Anjous. A precious monument of Hungarian art from the age of Andrew III is at the Historical Museum of Bern, namely the King's small private altar which his widow, Queen Agnes, presented to the monastery of Königsfeld (Switzerland) which she had founded in 1308. This masterpiece of the goldsmith's art was most probably made in Hungary in the last decade of the 13th century. It is particularly interesting that the small altarpiece is a diptych. The slightly ponderous and massive goldsmith's work, which is affixed to two thick panels, almost creates the impression of having been designed for the cover of a large manuscript; it certainly has something of the character of the ornamental work done by medieval goldsmiths for book covers. From the age of the House of Árpád no costly bindings in metal work studded with gems and beads have been found, nor is any such work known from the art of later centuries. The simple but artistic silver cover of the Szelepchényi Evangelistary adorned with splendid figured decoration but without any precious stones, is the only evidence that book covers decorated with goldsmith's work were in fact made in Hungary. On Andrew III's altarpiece, which is adorned with precious stones, there are forty-four miniatures painted on parchment and protected by crystal plates; they represent not only the Annunciation and scenes from the life of Christ, but also half-length pictures of saints, including Hungarian saints. Painted in Byzantine and Venetian style on a gold-leaf background and the haloes of the saints studded with pearls, these magnificent miniatures show a close relationship to the goldsmith's work; they were clearly made specially for the altarpiece to replace the usual enamel plaques. Presumably these miniatures were painted in Hungary at the court of Andrew III by an artist who had been trained in Italy; the excellence of his workmanship and achievement bear witness to the high standard of Hungarian art in the age of the House of Árpád.

THE ANJOU PERIOD
MINIATURE ART
OF THE HUNGARIAN TRECENTO

Hungarian art of the 14th century, the Hungarian Trecento, achieved its form under the reigns of our two Anjou kings. On the Hungarian throne Charles I became one of the leading figures of Central Europe; under his son, Louis I (the Great), Hungary became a power in Europe. Under the rule of the two Anjou sovereigns Arpadian civilization and culture came to full maturity, and the older Hungarian art which had gradually arisen in previous centuries now received inspiration from new trends and flowered in radiant splendour.

After the death in 1301 of Andrew III, the last king of the House of Árpád, Charles I came to Hungary, travelling from Naples to Buda. He was barely thirteen years old. Though his grandmother had been a Hungarian princess, his ancestors were French, and he had received an Italian education. But at the court of Buda he became a Hungarian. With the adaptability of adolescence he embraced Hungarian culture, and he preserved and handed on Arpadian traditions. Unlike later Hungarian monarchs of foreign extraction, the King made no attempt to impose upon the Hungarian court the culture of his land of origin. Both Charles I and his son, Louis I, reigned in the spirit of Arpadian Hungarian traditions: Ladislas I was for them an ideal figure; they strove to realize, while recognizing the character of their own age and the requirements of feudalism, the aims which the kings of the House of Árpád had set.

During the reign of Charles I (1308–1342) cultural life and art were strongly under the influence of the French spirit of the past. As in the time of the House of Árpád, the miniatures painted in the Hungarian monasteries still showed marked French characteristics. From the opening years of this century valuable data are available concerning the production of illuminated manuscripts in Hungary. There was at this time an important and flourishing workshop for the copying and illumination of manuscripts at the Carthusian monastery of Látókő (now Klaštorisko, Czechoslovakia). Here a certain Conrad prepared missals, graduals and breviaries, and we read that in 1307 he put in a petition begging to be relieved of his office as prior that he might "devote his life more freely and completely to intellectual work and the production of books". A Gradual (Budapest, EK Cod. lat. 34) prepared before 1334, from a monastic library of the Augustine order, contains interesting instructions regarding the preparation of antiphonaries and graduals: "Friars are instructed," it says, "to use in graduals, antiphonaries and nocturns square notes and to paint four lines, all in red, without black; letters are to be written clearly and separately, so that the appropriate letter shall stand above the right note, and lines are to be at a proper distance from one another, nor should the notes be pressed in from either side. Secondly: the utmost care must be taken that the same letters, notes, slurs and rests shall be used as in the corrected copy. Scribes must neither add nor omit anything. Thirdly: any book copied from a copy is to be carefully and diligently corrected, with due attention both to letters and notes, before the volume be bound or presented to the choir, lest these works should, as is common, be defective. This is also most necessary for pontifical books, breviaries and missals, as soon as they have been received. Lastly, when graduals, ordinaries and missals have been corrected as laid down above, friars are to discharge their duties in accordance with their contents."

It is clear, therefore, that a considerable number of manuscripts were copied at the time in the monasteries, and that these manuscripts were bound. The unknown monk finished his instructions with the following warning: "Do not entrust the writing of such works or music to secular persons as long as there are monks in the order who possess proficiency in this work. If there are none, they should be compelled by their superiors to learn the craft, since priests spoil whatever music or text they copy."

Thus illuminated manuscripts were prepared not only by monks, but also by secular priests. On the evidence of the legend of St Dominic, monks despised secular priests who studied in Paris and after finishing their studies aspired to high positions in the Church. Such men, it was thought, were damned because Satan had filled them with worldly vanity; and it is in this belief that the writer of the instructions from which we have quoted disparages the work of secular priests. It is surprising that in his detailed instructions the monk should have said nothing about the decoration and illumination of manuscripts, although the volume in which his admonitions are to be read is a Gradual of large format (437 × 286 mm), richly decorated and with coloured initials (Plate V). These are of an individual and peculiar style; they are composed of motifs which show French influence and are executed in several colours. Large initials continued

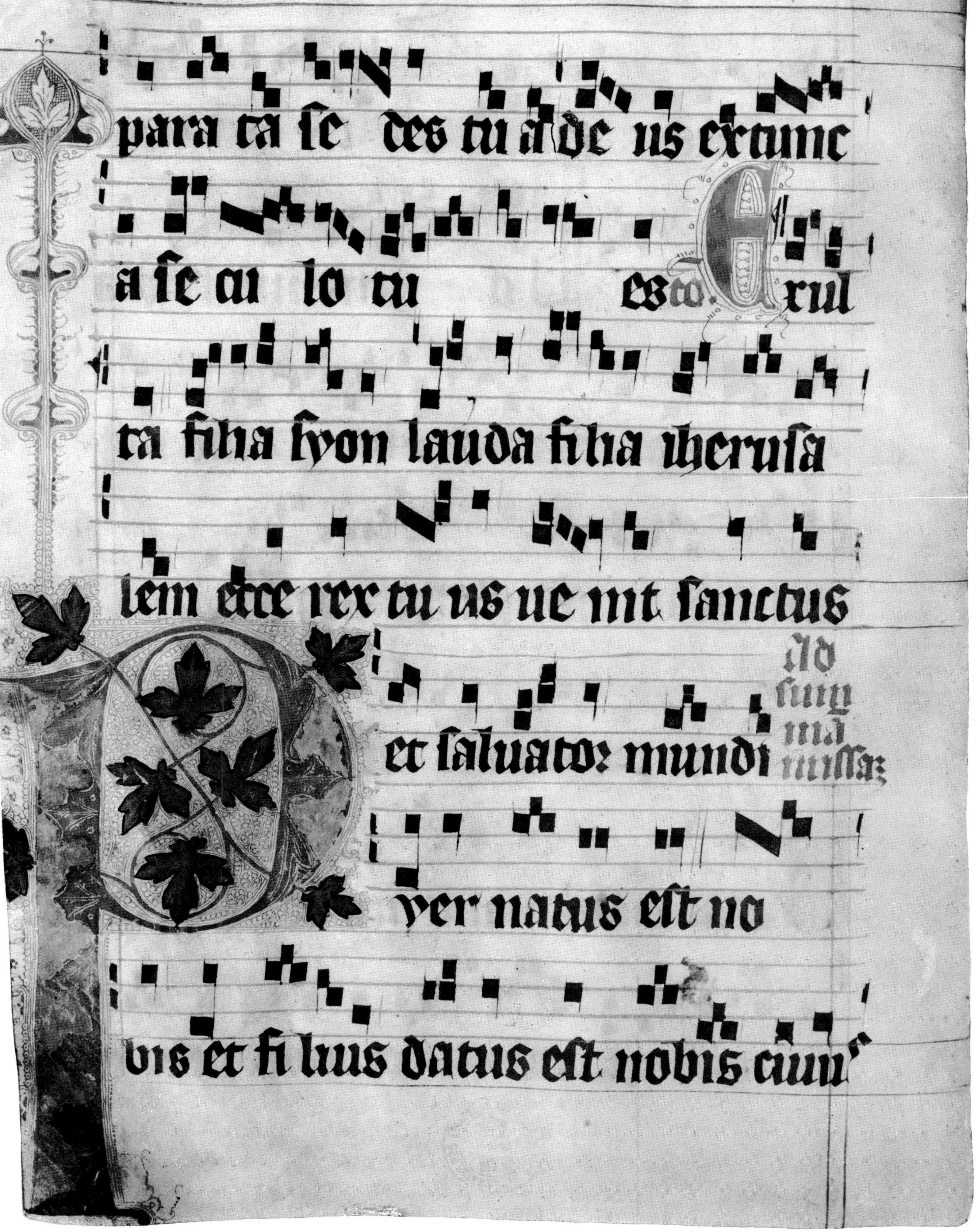
para ta se des tu a de us ex tunc
a se cu lo tu es. Exul
ta filia syon lauda filia iherusa
lem ecce rex tu us ue nit sanctus
et saluator mundi
uer natus est no
bis et fi lius datus est nobis cuius

4

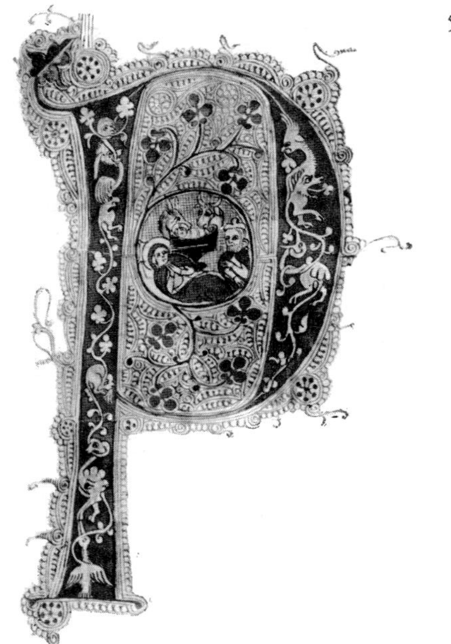

5

to develop the style of calligraphic design employed in the ornamentation of documents in the age of the House of Árpád. This large, elaborate Gradual has a counterpart of smaller size (280 × 210 mm; Budapest, EK Cod. lat. 35) with two initials executed in a similar style (Fig. 4).

Several antiphonaries from a Franciscan workshop also belong to this period, as does a Gradual of the Augustine order (Budapest, EK Cod. lat. 119, 121, 122 and 123). In these, however, the illumination has been carried out in the colours of calligraphy, in blue and minium, and the execution is rather more crude and clumsy. In these manuscripts we find drolleries in the French manner; they are executed with a very quaint wit, though the faces are very unlike those in their models (Fig. 5).

In the monastery at Pozsony (now Bratislava, Czechoslovakia) there was already flourishing in the 1330s a characteristic calligraphic miniature art, of which we possess examples in four Missals (Budapest, OSZK Clmae 94, 214, 220 and 435); one of them (Clmae 214) bearing the date 1341. This volume is decorated with small compositions executed with great delicacy and taste; the representation of the Nativity is particularly interesting (Plate VI; Figs. 6–9). In these Missals there are also a large and a smaller Canon in colour (Clmae 435, 220; Plates VII and VIII). The painting of Canon Tables, with representations of Christ on the Cross, had by this time become general in Hungarian miniature art. Several Canons painted in varying styles have survived in the missals painted in the middle of the century.

Side by side with French traits in the monastic miniature art of the first half of the century there is increasing evidence in the art of illumination of Hungary's cultural relations with Italy. Many Hungarians were at this time educated in Italy, especially at the famous university town of Bologna; as a result, illuminated manuscripts made in Italy found their way to Hungary, and not only illuminated manuscripts, but also miniaturists. Moreover, Hungarian artists trained in Italy may have returned to illuminate manuscripts in their native country. In the first years of the century a manuscript of modest execution, *Summa dictaminis* by Petrus de Vineis (Vienna, National Library Cod. 481), considered by Hungarian experts to be Neapolitan work, was in Hungarian possession. This manuscript is exceedingly plain: the text is written in one column, in cursive hand. On the title-page a small initial displays the author's half-length portrait. The initial is completed with plain border decoration con-

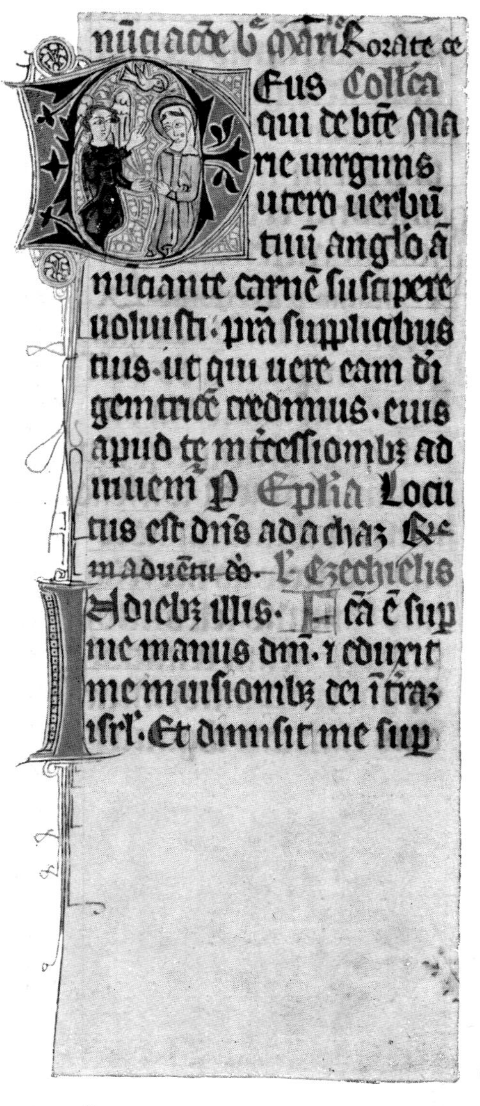

6

mee · et sit michi remis-
sio omnium peccatorum
meorum · Hic sumat san-
guinem et dicat · Sang-
uis domini nostri ihesu xpi
custodiat animam me-
am in uitam eternam
Amen · Postquam co-
mmunicauerit dicat:
Quod ore sumpsimus
domine pura mente capi-
amus · et de munere tem-
porali fiat nobis reme-
dium sempiternum ·
Corpus tuum domine
quod sumpsi et sanguis
quem potaui · adhe-
reat in uisceribus meis
et presta ut in me non re-
maneat scelerum macu-
la · quem pura et sancta
refecerunt sacramen-
ta · Qui viuis et reg-
nas cum deo patre in v-
nitate Explicit canon
In die Pasche offi[cium]

Resurrexi
et adhuc te-
cum sum
alleluia posuisti
super me
manum tuam
alleluia mirabilis facta est scien-
tia tua alleluia alleluia · ps Domine
probasti me et cognovisti · Gloria patri
Deus qui Oracio
hodierna die per
unigenitum tuum
eternitatis nobis adi-
tum deuicta morte
reserasti · uota nostra
que preueniendo aspi-
ras · etiam adiuuan-
do prosequere · Per eundem
Ad Corinthios
Fratres · Expurga-
te uetus fermen-
tum · ut sitis noua con-
spersio · sicut estis azi-
mi · Etenim pascha
nostrum ymmolatus est
xpc · Itaque epulemur

sisting of South Italian and other very small motifs. The manuscript is further illuminated with five small initials with some border decoration and a small calligraphic initial in red and blue. As the use of such calligraphic initials was general in Hungary, an Italian artist, or one who had studied in Italy, may have illuminated this manuscript in Hungary, so strikingly simple in execution. Charles I may also well have brought books with him from Italy, though no titles are at present known. There is, however, good reason to believe that the Erlangen Bible, which is Neapolitan work from the close of the 13th century and which was to be acquired by the Corvina Library, had belonged to Charles I. There is also written evidence that some members of the aristocracy and also prelates were bibliophiles. An illuminated manuscript was prepared for Jacob of Piacenza, one of Charles I's prelates at Avignon. Recent research has also identified a superbly illuminated Bible as having been in the possession of the Lord Chief Treasurer Demetrius Nekcsei.

Hungarian education had already earlier experienced the influence of Bologna. In the 13th century, more than sixty Hungarian students, so far as we know, had studied law at its university.

In the first half of the 14th century Hungarian students played an active part in the university life. In 1316 Nicolaus de Hungaria was elected leader, that is *rector*, of the student body; the new laws of the university were introduced while he was in office. In the 1320s Jacobus, guardian canon of Esztergom and archdeacon of Nógrád, also acted as rector at Bologna, though his tenure of office ended in a scandal. In 1321 a Spanish student wanted to elope with the daughter of a notary of Bologna and among his armed helpers there was a Hungarian student. The Spaniard undergraduate was executed, but the Hungarian escaped. Thereupon the Hungarian students, headed by the rector Jacobus, left Bologna without paying their debts and went to the University of Siena, where Jacobus filled the office of rector for two years. The town of Bologna, however, seized all the valuables left behind by Jacobus against his debts, including his books, among which were a splendid Bible, a handsome speculum, a decretal and other manuscripts.

Several illuminated manuscripts may have been brought to Hungary from Italy in this period. In Hungarian miniature painting in the first half of the century indications of the artist having received an Italian training become more noticeable, and the influence of the decorative motifs used in Italian miniature art makes itself increasingly felt. In this connection, close examination is particularly

xi.

mirati sunt · et de hiis que dicta e
rant a pastoribus ad ipsos · Ma
ria aūt conservabat omnia ūba
hec conferens in corde suo · Et
reūsi sunt pastores glorificā
tes et laudantes deū in omnibus
que audierant et viderant · sic
dictum est ad ipsos · Off. Deus
enim firmavit orbem terre qui nō cō
movebitur parata sedes tua ds ex tunc
a seculo tu es.
Munera Sec.
Nr̄a qs domine nativi
tatis hodierne mysteriis apta
proveniant · ut sicut homo geni
tus idem refulsit deus · sic nobis
hec terrena sbstancia cōferat qd
divinum est · P eūd · Secretum
Accipe qs dom̄e mun̄a dig
nanter oblata · et bte ana
stasie suffragantibus mitis · ad
nr̄e salutis auxilium provenire
cōcede · P · pphacō Qm̄e deus
Quia p incarnati ūbi · Con
municantes et diem sac̄ · Co · Ex
ulta filia syon lauda filia iherusalem
ecce rex tuus venit scūs et salvator mū
Huius nos dn̄e sa · Compl. · di
cramenti semp novitas
natalis instauret · cuius nativi
tas singularis humanam re

pulit vetustatem · Pe · Compl.
Faciasti dn̄e familiā tuam
muneribus sacris · eius qs se
per intuencōe nos refove · cuius
sollempnia celebramus · P · Offi.
Puer nat
est nobis et fi
lius datus ē
nobis cuius
imperiū sup
humerū eius
et vocabitur
nom̄ eius magni consilii angls · Ps. Li
Can tate dn̄o canticū novū quia mirabilia fecit
Dn oro.
Concede qs omnipc deus
ut nos unigeniti
tui nova p carnem nativitas
libet · quos sub peccati iugo ve
tusta s̄vitus tenet · Pe · Leccio
Hec dicit dn̄s · ysaie pphe
Propter hoc sciet pp̄ls
meus nom̄ meū in die illa · q̄a
ego ip̄e qui loquebar ecce adsum ·
Quam pulcri sup montes pe
des annūciantis et pdicantis pa
cem · annūciantis boni · pdicā
tis salutem dicentis · Syon · reg
nabit deus tuus · Vox specula
torum tuoꝶ levaverūt vocē · si
mul laudabunt · quia oculo ·

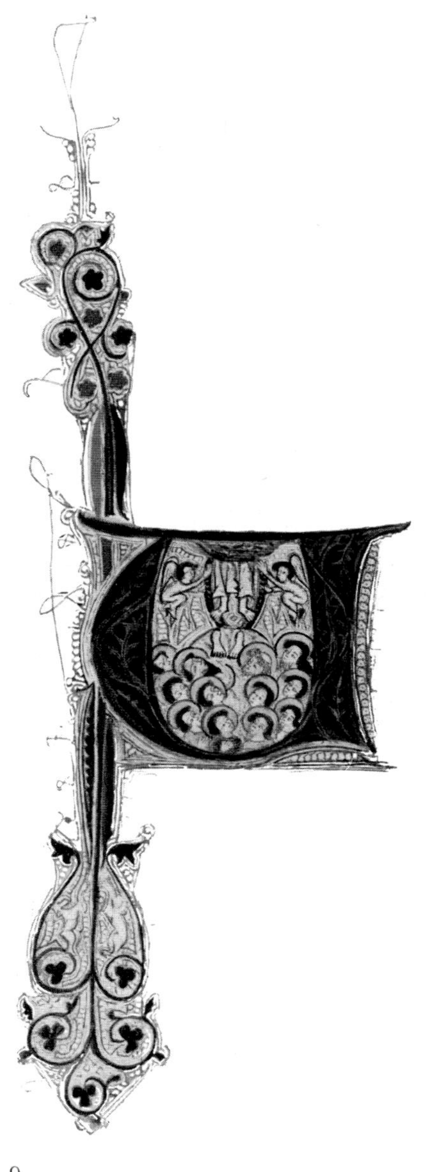

9

required of two richly illuminated manuscripts preserved at Padua (Cathedral Capitular Library Cod. A 24 and Cod. A 25), attributed to the Italian miniaturist Pseudo-Niccolò da Bologna. In the 1340s these volumes were in Hungarian possession, most likely in the library of Nicolaus Vásári, provost of Esztergom (1339–1347). One of them (Cod. A 25) is dated 1343. Cod. A 24 contains miniatures representing scenes from the life of St Stephen, King of Hungary.

The students of the University of Bologna, it may be remarked, again had a Hungarian rector in 1343 in the person of Johannes Uzsai of Veszprém. Presumably it was he who owned the decretal of Pope Boniface VIII, which included magnificent examples of the work of the most eminent miniaturist of Bologna, Niccolò di Giacomo da Bologna (1330–1402), painted when the artist was a young man (Vienna, National Library Cod. 2042).

This manuscript raises an interesting question. Only the last few pages (folios 116, 116v, and 117) were illuminated by Niccolò di Giacomo da Bologna with two highly ornate major miniatures and one minor figured initial. The other miniatures and initials of the manuscript were done by a less gifted artist who had been trained at Bologna, but whose technique was somewhat sketchy and perfunctory. One cannot help wondering, though we have no supporting evidence, whether these miniatures and initials may not have been done by a Hungarian master working or studying in the circle of Niccolò di Giacomo da Bologna, although the style shows more resemblance to that of the school preceding Giacomo da Bologna rather than to that of the master himself. A work executed in the 1330s for the Lord Chief Treasurer Demetrius Nekcsei in Hungary, a manuscript as splendid as the Washington Bible (Washington, Library of Congress, MS. Pre-Accession 1), makes this question all the more pertinent. The rich, artistic illumination of the Nekcsei Bible is related to the art of the excellent Bolognan miniaturist, Pseudo-Niccolò da Bologna, but its local Hungarian allusions suggest that the manuscript was produced in Hungary. The truly splendid execution of the Vatican Illuminated Legendary (Rome, Vatican Library, Cod. lat. 8541), a few severed leaves of which are in the Pierpont Morgan Library in New York, and a few also in the Ermitage in Leningrad, would also seem to point to Hungarian origin. Curiously enough, these two magnificent works are written not in the typical Bolognan *rotundo* hand, but in the Gothic majuscules used at the time in Hungary. The ornate miniatures of these two manuscripts indicate that in the first half of the 14th century Italian, particularly Bolognan, miniaturists were active in Hungary, presumably in a workshop maintained by the royal court. Here in this court workshop Italian conceptions were transmuted into Hungarian form; and this stylistic development was to be reflected in the great product of the secular culture of the Anjou period, the Illuminated Chronicle.

While they follow the typical and outstanding miniatures of Bolognan art, the miniatures of the Illuminated Legendary display a close affinity to the decorations of the Nekcsei Bible. Striking in their similarity of style and spirit, these two works exhibit elements which were later to recur in the Illuminated Chronicle, both in fundamental qualities of style and particularly in some ornamental motifs, as also in the definition of gestures and in a certain clumsiness in the attitudes. In the artistic excellence of the decorations the continuous progress of Hungarian miniature art in the Trecento is worthily illustrated.

Finished before Louis I was crowned King of Poland in 1370, the Illuminated Chronicle, *Chronica de Gestis Hungarorum* (Budapest, OSZK Clmae 404), is not only of the greatest significance for Hungarian history and literature; it is the monumental work of secular miniature art in the Anjou period. The illustrations were most probably painted by Nicolaus Meggyesi who, as is proved by old records, was the court painter and heraldic painter of King Louis I, and painted for him a pleasing variety of attractive pictures. His father, Master Hertul, had been the court painter of Charles I already in the 1320s. None of Master Hertul's known works has survived, but there can be no doubt that he was in contact with the royal workshop of miniaturists and with Italian masters, as well as with illuminators who having been trained in Italy were working in Hungary. Thus it was in an artistic centre with deep roots in Hungary that the son received his education.

The value of the miniatures adorning the Illuminated Chronicle lies not only in the high standard of their artistic workmanship. Since their subjects include scenes of worldly life, very rarely depicted at that time, these miniatures are a truly unique mirror of society in the Anjou period. Their painter had an observant eye and an unparalleled gift for depicting what he saw; while remaining within the narrow limits of miniature painting, through the selection and treatment of his themes he illuminated the social conditions and life at the court of Louis the Great. In his endeavour to portray reality truthfully, he painted the lives and fate of the kings and princes of the House of Árpád, of evil counsellors and intriguers, the heroism of the Hunga-

10

rians and the feats of valour performed by their kings. He represented heroic deeds, defeats, cruelty, blinding, bloodshed, regicide, and even painted an attempt on the life of Charles I (Plate XIII, Fig. 12). Apart from the Illuminated Chronicle, we have knowledge only of one modest achievement by the artist, namely the more plainly painted title-page of the Pseudo-Aristotelean manuscript *Secretum secretorum*, the second of the two books known to have belonged to King Louis I, now in Britain (Oxford, Bodleian Library).

The themes of the miniatures give the Illuminated Chronicle importance not only in the history of Hungarian art; it possesses international significance. In no other work of this age, so far as we know, are there to be found such vivid pictures of the world of feudalism. The development of commerce and the rise of bourgeoisie, the introduction of manufacture, and the sudden advance of the guilds called into being in Italy in the first half of the 14th century a new kind of secular painting; the new tendencies found expression in miniatures representing trade and everyday life.

The miniaturist of the Illuminated Chronicle must have been familiar with Italian manuscripts and their representations of social life. In many countries at this time, and also, as recent research has shown, in Hungary, numerous romances and tales of chivalry were written, often illustrated with pictures of battles. Their influence is clearly discernible in the art of the master of the Illuminated Chronicle; but, contrary to the art of his day, and especially to trends in the tales of chivalry, the miniaturist of the Illuminated Chronicle made no attempt to portray the luxurious trapping of the age, the courtly life of knights, the pomp and festivities. It is characteristic of the Hungarian master's art that his work is uninfluenced by the poetry of the feudal age of chivalry or by lyrical love poetry in general.

Except when they evoke scenes of ancient myth and legend, the miniatures of the Illuminated Chronicle do not depict a serene world. The events of Hungarian history and the selfishness of feudalism are represented by the miniaturist in a sombre, tragic tone. The work of this Hungarian master not only ranks with the contemporary art of other countries, but in many respects it is in advance of it, so extraordinary are the themes of his miniatures. At the same time in the artistic quality of his miniatures we find that power of expression which characterizes the monumental art, the fresco paintings and the sculpture of the Anjou period in Hungary.

Other works of ecclesiastical and sacred character from the middle and the second half of the 14th century also show how certain motifs

Suscipe sancta trinitas hanc oblacionem quam tibi offerimus
ob memoriam passionis resurrectionis et ascensionis domini
nostri ihesu cristi et in honore beate marie semper virginis et
beati iohannis baptiste et istorum apostolorum Petri et pauli et istorum
omnium sanctorum ut illis proficiat ad honorem nobis autem ad salutem
et illi omnes pro nobis intercedere dignentur in celis quorum memoriam
agimus in terris. Per dominum nostrum ihesum cristum filium

of Italian miniature painting were absorbed into Hungarian miniature art. In two beautiful border decorations of Wenceslas Ganois's Bible (Budapest, OSZK Clmae 78) the miniaturist pleases himself by introducing into Italian interlacings lively human figures in the manner of the Italian Trecento—a King David dressed as a Hungarian king of the Anjou period touching the strings of his lute (Plate XII), or a long-bearded figure which may be interpreted as God the Father. Italian influence may be traced also in the miniatures of the precious Missal of Pozsony (Budapest, OSZK Clmae 215). This manuscript was illuminated with bold artistic power and freedom by the miniaturist known as the Master of The Agony of Christ. The border decoration in Italian style and the bird motifs (fol. 20, fol. 125, Plate IX), the remarkable representation of King David, iconographically noteworthy (fol. 8v; Fig. 10), the picture of The Agony of Christ (fol. 178; Plate X), and the large Crucifixion (fol. 178v; Plate XI) bear witness to highly developed artistic talent and individual conception. The Canons in missals representing Christ on the Cross followed at this time also in Hungary a well-defined type. An interesting drawing of Calvary may be found in a Missal prepared at Sopron in 1363, in the manuscript of Stephanus Galsó of Sopron (Budapest, OSZK Clmae 91). This miniature remained unfinished and uncoloured, but its delicate design testifies to the artistic excellence and variety of style with which Hungarian miniatures represented Calvary (Fig. 11).

The finest example of manuscripts executed for ecclesiastical purposes produced in Hungary in the age of Louis I, a Missal (Alba Iulia, Batthyanaeum R II. 134) was copied and painted in 1377 by the parish priest of Csukárd, Henry, for the guardian-canon of Pozsony, Johannes, the son of Emericus. It is worthy of note that the miniaturist Henry interspersed the small biblical scenes of the initials with tiny pictures of worldly subjects, for instance a young man playing the organ, or a naked woman sitting in the stocks, represented with expressive realism. The illumination of a Pontifical (Vienna, National Library Cod. lat. 1799) with motifs in the Italian manner is most probably also a product of provincial miniature art in Italian style from the 1370s. In the 16th century this manuscript was the property of Franciscus Várday, Bishop of Transylvania (1514–1524).

The great king of the Hungarian Trecento, Louis I, died in 1382. His successor to the crown was his daughter Maria. Within a few years of her accession, her husband, Sigismund of Luxembourg, the son of Charles IV, Holy Roman Emperor and King of Bohemia, who had

Anno dni M. ccc. Quinquagesimo octauo. feria tercia infra octauas Ascensionis dominice domini. Incepta e ista Cronica. de gestis hungarorum. antiquis et nouissimis. ortu et progressu uictoria eorundem q audatia. collecta ex diuersis Cronicis ueteribus. eandem ueritates ascribendo. q falsitatem omnino refutando. Anno inime domini ame. Incipit prolog in Cronicam hungarorum.

Per me reges regnat. Ait dominus deus p sapientem salomonem prouerbior. viii.

Capitulo. Gloriosus deus in sanctis suis in maiestate mirabilis. cuius ineffabilis altitudo prudentie. nullis inclusa limitibus. nullis terminis q prefixa. rerum censura iudicii celestis pariter disponit et firmat. Et sicuti eos ministros magnificet et altis tradet honoribus. q celebres efficit dignitatis possessores. illos tamen ut dignus digna rependantur ... cionibus attollit insignius dignitatum et principum uberiori retributione prosequitur. quos dignosciat agnoscit et commendat ingenio excellentia meritorum. sicut apparet luculentissime in excellentia regum illustrium et uictoriam exercitio celebrassimarum pregis hungarorum patratarum. Qui omnino freti auctoritatis presidio gladiorum acie be ualidissime p[er]fugatis. Castra subiicientes regum et imperatorum:

been educated at the court of Louis I, already shared the throne with his consort and after her death in 1395 he became King of Hungary in his own right.

The close of the 14th century marks a time of transition in Hungarian miniature painting. Not later than 1389, a Missal was made at Pozsony or Kassa (Budapest, OSZK Clmae 395), the illumination of which still shows Italian influences, but the forms are strongly modified by Hungarian taste. Among interlacings and Trecento scrolls, executed with a more animated rhythm, are to be seen the head of Judas, swine, oxen, birds and vases. In addition to Italian influences, in the badly damaged picture of Calvary the typically French golden, pink and green chequered network forming the simple background points to the continuance of French influence from the early Anjou period (Plate XIV). The development in Hungarian miniature painting at the end of the century is illustrated by a simpler Breviary of smaller size (Budapest, EK Cod. lat. 36). The illumination of this Breviary is believed to have been done by monks of the Premonstratensian order, most likely at Jászó (now Jasov, Czechoslovakia), after 1389. The miniatures inserted into the five initials of the manuscript and its border decorations foreshadow the trends which were to become dominant in the next fifty years in miniature art. Italian ornamental elements of the Trecento are here already interwoven with the Gothic foliated and floral scroll which had for some time been widely used in Bohemian and Austrian art and was to gain increasing favour in Hungarian miniature painting in the first half of the 15th century (Plate XV).

In the last decade of the 14th century, in 1394, a Hungarian miniaturist—his name, Ladislaus of Miskolc, is known—painted in a Missal a Canon with a picture of Christ on the Cross (Eger, Archiepiscopal Library U 2. VI. 5; Fig. 13). Though badly damaged, the miniature bears testimony to the fine talents of its painter. In the movement of the figure of the Holy Virgin, which has a certain Gothic intensity, and the calm, noble carriage of John one can feel the striving to give to the forms and idioms of ancient Hungarian art a heightened simplicity of expression. Christ's face is full of pain and suffering; blood flows from his wounds, and in the muscles of his arms and legs there is tension. The representation is realistic, but Ladislaus of Miskolc did not distort realism by carrying it to excess; neither did the painter of the Agony of Christ, in the Missal of Pozsony, during the reign of Louis I.

13

At the end of the 14th century, in the opening years of King Sigismund's reign, Hungarian miniature art showed clear signs of turning away from Trecento trends. The appearance of Gothic foliated scroll was accompanied by a change in the themes and content of miniatures. In the last years of the century miniature painting lost interest in representing Hungarian saints and the saintly heroic kings venerated in the Anjou period, and preferred more general religious compositions with themes from the Old and New Testaments, especially scenes of Calvary. The popularity at this time of miniatures representing the Crucifixion and Christ on the Cross is confirmed by the fact that two eminent artists of the northern parts of the country later decorated town minute-books for secular use with scenes of Calvary corresponding to the Canons of missals; in 1426 the minute-book of Körmöcbánya was thus decorated, and in 1432 that of Selmecbánya (now Kremnica, resp. Banská Štiavnica, Czechoslovakia).

MINIATURE PAINTING IN THE AGE OF SIGISMUND AND IN THE LATE GOTHIC PERIOD

Sigismund (1387–1437) was the first Hungarian monarch who was not only King of Hungary but also Holy Roman Emperor. An ambitious, passionate politician, not content with the crown of Stephen I, he finally became the possessor of five crowns. Besides ruling his German kingdom, he became King of Bohemia, then of Lombardy, and in the last years of his reign Emperor, Sovereign of the Holy Roman Empire. It was not by battles, but by his extraordinary gift for diplomacy that Sigismund conquered Europe and became the leading figure in European politics. He mediated between the monarchs of other countries, overthrew three popes, put an end to schism, sent John Huss to the stake, and waged a merciless war against the Hussites and against peasant revolts. To the end of his life he remained unpopular in Hungary.

That Sigismund possessed five kingdoms was a disadvantage to Hungary, but the fact that for years on end he stayed in his other realms brought benefit. The Hungarians in his retinue came into direct contact with western civilizations, and thus knowledge of new movements was brought back to the country not only by the few Hungarian students who were educated at Paris, Prague, Cracow, or Bologna; many hundreds of Hungarians now had personal experience of life in Germany, France and Spain. At the universities of other countries there were not only considerable numbers of Hungarian students and *rectors*, but also professors; moreover, many Hungarian artists worked abroad. Foreign artists also came to Hungary; there is evidence that during his stay in France, Sigismund engaged the services of the miniaturist Perrin, though this master is known to us only by name.

Sigismund had deep respect for scholars, as shown by his famous answer to Georgius Fiscellus at Basel in 1433 when the latter demanded that the seats of scholars should be given to nobles. "You act very foolishly, Georgius, and you make yourself ridiculous," he said, "if you show more respect for nobles than for scholars; I can knight a thousand ignorant men in one day, but I cannot create a single doctor in a thousand years." (Sigismund's witty retort was recorded by Aeneas Sylvius.)

In the court of Buda, too, there was a growing spirit of humanism. In the opening years of the 15th century a new form of art came into vogue at the royal chancellery, namely the ornate painting of letters patent granting armorial bearings. It is hardly possible today to form a clear picture of how miniature painting was practised at the court of Sigismund at Buda. Presumably there were miniaturists active at the court and illuminated books were prepared for the King whose brother Wenceslas, King of Bohemia, was a renowned bibliophile and kept several miniaturists busy at his court in Prague. Yet hardly any of this monarch's illuminated manuscripts are known to posterity, and only a single valuable piece of his collection is in Hungary, the *Liber de septem signis*, containing eight pen-and-ink drawings painted in water-colour (Budapest, Library of the Hungarian Academy of Sciences, Cod. lat. 2° 14). The miniaturist of this ornate manuscript painted Sigismund as the Sun, and his second wife, Barbara of Cilli, as the planet Venus. That the artist should have painted King Sigismund as the Sun becomes understandable on reading the first lines of the patents of nobility in which the sovereign compared the royal throne and power to the Sun: "The aristocracy with its legal prerogatives springs forth from the radiance of the royal throne as do the beams from the Sun; every title of nobility has its source in Royal Majesty, therefore it can originate only from the King's throne . . ." The illumination of the volume is described in the relevant literature as the work of a South German artist from the region of the Lake of Constance. It is quite possible, however, that the manuscript was executed at Buda. Future research into the history of Hungarian art must answer this question and also undertake a more thorough study of other magnificently illuminated manuscripts of Sigismund—and of his grandson, Ladislas V—which are preserved in other countries.

The *Liber de septem signis* is evidence of a lively interest in illuminated manuscripts at the court of King Sigismund. Yet we know hardly anything about his library although he inherited the splendid library of his elder brother Wenceslas, King of Bohemia and Holy Roman Emperor. It is, however, known that after the death of Sigismund's successor, the Hungarian King Albert who reigned only two years (1437–1439), the Emperor Frederick III removed 110 volumes which were part of the inheritance of Albert's posthumous son, the Hungarian King Ladislas V, from Buda to Wiener Neustadt. Some of these volumes were brought back to Hungary during the reign of Ladislas V (1452–1457), but the remains of Sigismund's library are still in the National Library of Vienna, and the illuminated manuscripts of Ladislas V are also in other countries.

Three manuscripts, which are in the National Library of Vienna, were illuminated by the excellent and mysterious "Martinus Opifex"; a Breviary (Cod. 1767), a magnificently decorated specimen of a German version of Guido de Columna's work, *Historia Troyana* (Cod. 2773), and Jacobus de Voragine's volume, the *Legenda aurea* (Cod. 326). Another splendid work by the same miniaturist, in the University Library of Granada, the richly decorated *Historia naturalis* of Albertus Magnus, has so far been discussed only very briefly in the relevant literature; mention was made in 1938 of further works known to be at Stuttgart and Gotha, but they have not been made the subject of any special study.

The illumination of the Breviary and the *Legenda aurea* of Vienna was not the work of Martinus Opifex alone. Other artists working at Frederick III's court at Vienna in 1447—the eminent miniaturist Michael, who was active when Ladislas V was a child, also a miniaturist referred to as Albrecht, King Albert's miniaturist, and his pupils—all contributed richly decorative work to the volumes.

There is nothing written in these two manuscripts and in the *Historia Troyana* to prove that they were the property of Sigismund, but allusions to Hungary make it evident that originally these volumes were made for Sigismund. On the ornate title-page of the Breviary, King Sigismund and his consort, Barbara of Cilli, are represented in the company of the six electors; scholars have suggested that this miniature was made to commemorate the meeting of the electors at Pozsony (1429). According to Hungarian experts on the subject, the *Legenda aurea* was also made for Sigismund, because in the original text of this collection no legend of any Hungarian saint is included except that of Elizabeth, whereas the Vienna Manuscript contains also the legends of St Stephen and St Ladislas. As regards the *Historia Troyana*, it is traditionally supposed that it was originally prepared for the Queen, Barbara of Cilli, who liked naughty stories.

In recent literature in other countries the art of Martinus Opifex has been considered as belonging to that of the circle of court miniature painting at Vienna. The master himself is regarded as the miniaturist of Frederick III, active in Vienna from 1445 to 1450, although in Austrian painting in the first half of the 15th century no parallel can be found to his style. Suida was the first to stress how solitary the art of Martinus stands in Austria. In his view Martinus's style points to French-Burgundian relationships, and his elaborate decorations,

14a

steeped in the spirit of the Late Gothic, continue the style of the Limbourg brothers. (It is an indication of the remarkable quality of Martinus's art that Suida should attribute to him the large St Barbara altar of Breslau, painted in 1447.)

In Hungarian works on the history of art Martinus Opifex has always been held to have been the court miniaturist of King Sigismund. These two different—but perhaps not contradictory—views are explained by several circumstances. Albert's posthumous son and Sigismund's grandson, who later became King Ladislas V of Hungary, was educated at the court of Frederick III in Vienna. As the guardian of Ladislas V, Frederick III not only had the books of Sigismund and Albert removed from Buda, but also took into his employment at his court in Vienna the artists who had worked for Sigismund and King Albert.

The excellent and prolific miniaturist Michael, who later illuminated the books of Ladislas V at Vienna, had also worked for Sigismund. During the reign of Sigismund, from 1427 to 1429, this miniaturist illuminated the work of Henricus de Secusia at Klosterneuburg, collaborating with the Hungarian Petrus de Lebeta, the copyist of the manuscript (Klosterneuburg, Capitular Library, Ms. 97). In 1436 Michael painted for Sigismund two magnificently decorated letters patent of the town of Pozsony. Whether he painted them at Klosterneuburg, in Vienna, at Buda or in Pozsony we do not know; but we may assume that they were prepared in the immediate entourage of Sigismund. The style of the miniaturist Michael differed considerably from that of Martinus Opifex. Michael was an artist of Klosterneuburg: his work exhibits Austrian Gothic features. In the quivering, flowing folds of their garments his slender, elongated figures become incorporeal and ethereal. Martinus Opifex's fresh conception of nature, on the other hand, heralded the coming of the Renaissance to Sigismund's court, bringing the spirit of realism and of the new strivings in art.

In the history both of Hungarian and of Austrian miniature painting the personality of Martinus has remained an enigma. His œuvre is not completely known, nor is it certain when and where he was active. The biographical material is obscure and his name is mysterious. It is encountered only once, on the title-page of the German version of Guido de Columna's *Historia Troyana*. In the centre of the page beneath the German text, within the marginal illumination, "Martinus Opifex" is written in golden letters similar to those used in the text. But does this name really refer to the miniaturist? Miniaturists were not, in fact, in the habit of calling themselves "opifex" and they never signed their works thus. May not this have been the name of a scribe or a translator? It is, in any event, remarkable that the inscription "Martinus Opifex" occurs only this once, on the title-page of a volume containing the manuscript of a German translation, and the representation of a scholar in the initial may perhaps be the portrait of the translator whose name is omitted from the text of the manuscript, and who may have been a well-known personality in the entourage of King Sigismund. Until now no study of the *Historia Troyana* of Vienna has been undertaken with the purpose of identifying the translator of the text. It has been suggested that it is by no means certain that the name "Martinus Opifex" is that of the eminent miniaturist, but until the question has been elucidated by new researches we continue to follow the accepted usage in the relevant literature and to refer to him by the name of Martinus Opifex. Since it is to be expected that the art of Martinus Opifex will arouse continually growing interest among research workers, it will not be out of place to consider here his art in some detail.

The *Historia Troyana* is one of the master's most remarkable works, not only on account of the peculiar charm of the worldly subjects represented in its miniatures, but also because the nine initials and 333 miniatures of the manuscript were all painted by the artist himself. (A little-known manuscript to be seen in Granada, also illuminated with splendid miniatures on worldly themes, is also his work.) Judging from their relation to the development and changes in the artistic style of Martinus Opifex, the miniatures of the *Historia Troyana* may be regarded as the earliest of the master's identified works. Martinus drew his characters with vivid imagination and realism; their gestures are bold; the thick-set figures, sometimes somewhat clumsy, are full of animation, and all the innumerable happenings of life are truthfully depicted. The face of Priam's dead son, Hector, is livid, the eye-sockets sunken; around him stand the wailing mourners, some with arms raised high and others tearing their hair 14b
(fol. 224). In another miniature preparations are made to besiege Troy: a Greek setting up a tent drives a tent-peg into the ground with a powerful blow (fol. 168). The Greeks unloading their ships, walk along a plank laid across a small boat, carrying heavy chests and sacks on their shoulders (fol. 58). Besides depicting the rhythms of the work of everyday life in the time of Sigismund, the miniatures also convey a sense of the glitter and pomp of the court and of its sports and pastimes. Attended by Trojans, Paris and the lovely Helen

ride to celebrate the feast of Venus on the Island of Cythera; Helen (Barbara of Cilli?) is dressed in gold, and on her outstretched right hand a grey falcon may be seen. The distinguished ladies and gentlemen of her retinue are attired in clothes of golden brocade. In front rides the fool on a brown horse, with a large grey monkey on his back (fol. 105).

The highly individual style of Martinus's art is not easily related to the various schools of miniature painting of his time. His fresh realism points partly to Burgundy; it is impossible to overlook in his works features which are kindred to the art of the two great masters of the Burgundian court, the brothers van Eyck. Some of the representations in the *Historia Troyana* recall the pale glimmer of the miniatures attributed to Hubert van Eyck in one of the manuscripts of Turin, which were damaged by fire—for example, the shipwreck of Ajax, son of Oileus (fol. 357), where drowning men desperately clutch at the wreckage, while the sparkling spray is tossed from the white-crested waves of the angry sea. Yet the remarkable power of expression exhibited in the works of Martinus Opifex and his style cannot be related only to contemporary miniature painting; it has much more in common with the style of that equally mysterious and individualistic painter, Konrad Witz. Eminent artist though he was, comparatively few of his works have survived, except the panels painted in the last decade of his life, and we have no certain knowledge that he actually did paint miniatures or illuminate manuscripts.

In the Hungarian literature on the subject, Edit Hoffmann assumed that Martinus Opifex had been trained in Burgundy and pointed briefly to an affinity of style to that of Konrad Witz from Rottweil, an outstanding personality of the Early Renaissance and also inspired by Burgundian art. From the evidence of contemporary records, Konrad Witz was active from 1434 until his death in 1447, working at Basel and Geneva. Notwithstanding certain differences, the miniatures of the *Historia Troyana*—and also those of the Granada manuscript—display such an astonishing similarity of traits and motifs with the art of Witz that it would not be amazing if a historian of art with bold imagination were to discover in these miniatures evidence of the hand of Konrad Witz and to consider them to be early works by him.

In the painting of panels and of miniatures there have always been certain differences of execution, technique and artistic aim; and the differences may be felt in the case of the miniatures of Martinus Opifex and the panels of Konrad Witz. At the same time, the work of the two artists shows striking resemblances in their extremely realistic conception of nature and in their use of favourite motifs. The realism and the extraordinarily individual character of Witz's art—the movement of the fishermen in his picture Christ Walking on the Water, where the landscape can be identified as a particular stretch of shore of the Lake of Geneva—we find also in the brilliant realistic painting of some of the scenes of the *Historia Troyana* and the manuscript of Granada.

15

Incidentally, in the representation of gesture and movement in the manuscript of Granada there is a popular and grotesque element which is all the more remarkable in that these scenes were painted about a century before the pictures of the elder Pieter Bruegel.

In the treatment of landscape curious resemblances may be traced between the miniatures of the *Historia Troyana* and some pictures of Konrad Witz. Though the landscapes of the miniatures, being painted in dilute colours, are more sketchily executed, they show in the treatment of rocks and the painting of seascapes and lakes a definite, unmistakable relationship to the backgrounds of Witz's Crucifixion, St Christopher, and Christ Walking on the Water. In his picture of St Christopher he painted in the foreground a reedy marsh with cat's-tail pointing skyward. It is interesting to note that the miniaturist of the *Historia Troyana* also showed a liking for this unusual motif. In one instance, on a shore with white ripples, seven small heads of reed-mace rise above the shorter, now rather faded, green bulrushes (fol. 33v). In another instance, two white storks are standing before ten heads of reed-mace on a small island of sedge, with deep water beyond (fol. 95). A similar motif may be found in a picture of the Hermit St Anthony and the Hermit St Paul, dated 1445, which is at Donaueschingen; this work is supposed to have been painted by an unknown artist of Basel who worked in the immediate circle of Witz. (It may be added that also in its general effect this work shows a close affinity to the art of Martinus Opifex.)

The painting of buildings, towns and fortified castles in the *Historia Troyana* is also related to the art of Witz. Similarities may also be observed with the works of the master regarded as a follower of Konrad Witz, and referred to as the Master of Sierentz, the painter of St George and St Martin on horseback. These two panels, to be seen in the museum at Basel, are assumed to have been painted around 1450.

It is not only in the miniatures of the *Historia Troyana* that Martinus Opifex uses rich landscape backgrounds; they also enliven the splendid but slightly hieratic religious compositions of the Vienna

16

17

Breviary—as one example we may mention the landscape stretching into the distance in the Visit to the Sepulchre (fol. 108v).

On the title-page of the Vienna Breviary, as we have already mentioned, the miniaturist painted the portraits of Sigismund and Barbara of Cilli. In the *Historia Troyana* there is also a characteristic representation of Sigismund painted with strict observance of the symbolical representations of royalty. It is a notable achievement of recent Hungarian literature on the history of art to have identified this portrait through research into the iconography of representations of Sigismund in the art of Masolino. As already observed, the miniature in the first initial of the *Historia Troyana* represents a scholar reading in a book which he is holding. The second miniature of the manuscript represents, in illustration of the text, King Peleus with his consort, Queen Thetis, and Achilles (fol. 2). There can be no doubt that in this miniature the king is Sigismund, and the queen Barbara of Cilli (Fig. 24). It is not without interest that this portrait of Sigismund with the characteristic tall hat and the expressive gesture of the hand may be identified also in the picture by Konrad Witz of King David and the kneeling Abishai, painted for the *Heilspiegelaltar*, now in the museum at Basel. The King Peleus of the miniature and the King David of the painting present symbolically in an almost identical manner the mighty Hungarian King and Holy Roman Emperor.

Beside the worldly pictures of the *Historia Troyana*, the twenty-eight miniatures on sacred themes in the Vienna Breviary shed further light on the art of Martinus Opifex. Executed with great artistic skill and assurance, these religious compositions are the work of an experienced painter of great erudition. This is shown in the marvellously realistic floral frame decoration of the Annunciation (fol. 79v), and in the Entombment where, as a sign of Renaissance predilection for sharp contrasts, in the border decoration framing the dramatic scene there is the figure of a laughing court jester—the counterpart to the grotesque fool in the *Historia Troyana* (fol. 257). These two miniatures of the Breviary are the most mature works of Martinus Opifex.

The third manuscript in which traces of Martinus Opifex's work may be recognized, the *Legenda aurea*—like the Vienna Breviary—was illuminated also by Michael, as well as by the miniaturist referred to as Albrecht, who was his pupil at the court of Frederick III in 1447–48. The research worker who comes to this volume with the high expectations aroused by the art of Martinus Opifex is undeniably disappointed. Most of the miniatures attributed to the artist seem superficial and sketchy in execution, as if the hand that painted them had been tired and lifeless; they may well have been done, not by the great master himself, but by one of his followers and imitators. It is possible that in 1447 Martinus Opifex worked together with Michael and the miniaturist Albrecht in Vienna at the court of Frederick III. It is equally possible, however, that the *Legenda aurea* was produced in Vienna in 1447, and that the Breviary which the artist had begun earlier at the order of Sigismund was completed there in the same year, but only after the death of Martinus Opifex.

A true evaluation of the art of Martinus Opifex will only be possible when his still unknown works have been identified and studied—a task which has awaited historians of art for over twenty-five years. Study of the hieroglyphs—they may perhaps be secret monograms—which are sometimes used as ornamental motifs in the miniatures of the *Historia Troyana* may help towards gaining closer knowledge of his mysterious personality.

A curious figured motif in a badly worn letters patent furnishes proof that the highly significant art of Martinus Opifex did not remain without influence in Hungary. It is the letters patent dated December 23, 1434, in Pozsony, conferred by King Sigismund on Dionysius of Kistárkány, in which a barefooted man in a shirt, originally white, now grey, is wrestling with a wolf on the dark-blue ground of the shield, which is framed with gold. The bearded man has stabbed the rearing wolf in the throat with his dagger, and he is now fighting it with his bare hands: with his left hand he grips the wolf's mouth and hanging tongue, with his right he has seized a front leg. On his face there are the marks of bleeding wounds (Fig. 25). No similar representation of such a figure has been found on any of the letters patent from the Sigismundian era, or in contemporary provincial miniature painting.

We find this man, however, in the miniatures of Martinus Opifex, as an aristocrat or a Greek warrior. The stiff attitude of the man's straddling legs, the painting of the long feet, the ears, the hair and the wide loose sleeves and the folds of the shirt all point to a follower of Martinus's art. The bearded head resembles the types of face painted by Martinus, but the artistic workmanship indicates a weaker hand. Most probably the figure was painted in the Martinus circle and is the work of an assistant, a pupil or a follower. The influence of Martinus's realistic background landscapes was to become noticeable later in 15th-century Hungarian panel painting.

18

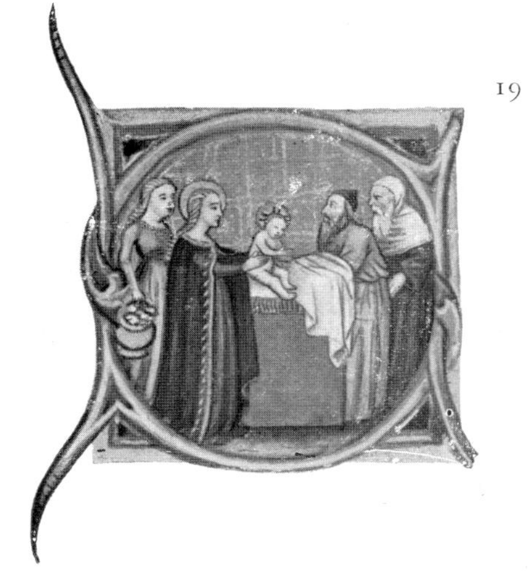

19

20

Although few books have come down to posterity from Sigismund's royal library of Buda, there is evidence of advanced literary culture outside the royal residence, and a number of beautiful volumes prove how high were the standards of miniature art and how widely it was practised. Several ornate illuminated manuscripts of Georgius Pálóczy, Archbishop of Esztergom (1423–1439), have survived, and Nicolaus III, Bishop of Vác, who employed a miniaturist at his court, Master Johannes of Vác, must also have been an important book-lover.

The surviving Hungarian provincial miniatures from Sigismund's age are the works of masters known by name—Ladislaus of Miskolc, who has already been mentioned, also Michaelis de Tyrnavia, Valentinus Gobil of Selmec, and the anonymous miniaturist known as the Master of Körmöcbánya.

Michaelis de Tyrnavia was active in the years about the turn of the century in Pozsony, where he was canon from 1381 to 1403. Two elaborate Missals of his are known; one is in Budapest (OSZK Clmae 216), the other used to be in Pozsony, in the Capitular Library; a present nothing is known of its whereabouts.

The name of the miniaturist was inscribed in both volumes and in the last lines of the Pozsony Missal even the date of the manuscript is given: *Iste liber est completus per manus domini Michaelis de Tyrnavia canonici Posoniensis ad laudem dei omnipotentis. Sub anno domini 1403.* The title-pages of the two Missals were almost entirely similar, with only minor differences. In the initial *A* King David may be seen praying before an altar. Disregarding the taste of his age, the artist did not decorate the altar with Gothic tracery and instead of a Gothic vaulting he painted a flat Italian coffered ceiling, following the traditions of Anjou miniature painting which made use of harmonious Italian architectural elements (Plate XVI). These may be found also in Hungarian panel painting, and again in the diptych of Bát (now Batovce, Czechoslovakia) from the end of the 14th century, also in the Annunciation from the early 15th century in the Museum of Košice. The relationship of Michaelis de Tyrnavia's miniatures to Hungarian panels may be recognized also in some of the types of faces: those seen in the Missal of Budapest, particularly the head of John the Baptist, recall the representation of the bearded figure on the diptych of Bát.

The border decorations of Michaelis de Tyrnavia were Trecento in character, as was the floral ornamentation of the Premonstratensian Breviary made around 1390, mentioned earlier. In the scrolls of the

Missals nodes of Italian style may still be found, but instead of the stylized leaves of the Trecento there is a feeling of life and sap in its foliage. The drops of gold restlessly winding through this foliated scroll ornament already betray the influence of Bohemian and Austrian miniature art, contrary to Italian taste. In Hungarian illuminated manuscripts this increasingly restless interlacing of foliated scrolls became a characteristic feature of Gothic miniature painting. Coming into use in the time of Sigismund, it remained obligatory until it was superseded by the Renaissance art of Matthias's court.

21

Two Hungarian miniaturists are known from the end of the 14th century. Clerk Bernard and Thomas Temlinus illuminated a Bible and Ockham's *Directorium iuris* (Vienna, National Library Cod. 2146 and Cod. 1215) at Esztergom in 1394; the simple decorations of these two modestly illuminated manuscripts have been torn out long ago by the hands of vandals.

In the series of manuscripts painted in the provinces in the reign of Sigismund there is a gap of about twenty years. Only from the 1420s do we again know of illuminated manuscripts with decorations by eminent artists. The third decade of the 15th century is significant not only in regard to Hungarian miniature painting but also to the history of Hungarian art in general. At this time the first Hungarian panel painter known by name, Thomas de Coloswar, was active; it was he who painted the famous altarpiece of Garamszentbenedek in 1427, which opened a new era in Hungarian art. In miniature painting also at this time a new conception made itself felt; excellent miniatures, painted in the spirit of the Garamszentbenedek altarpiece have survived. The Anonymous Master of Körmöcbánya (1426) and Valentinus Gobil of Selmec (1432) were active in the same period as Thomas de Coloswar; their paintings were inspired with a similar artistic conception and they employed similar means of expression. A good many years earlier, however, Master Johannes, the miniaturist of the Bishop of Vác (1423), and the artist of Pozsony who was the heraldic painter of the letters patent of Kassa (1423), had also found means of expression similar to those applied by Thomas de Coloswar in his monumental triptych.

In the year 1423 Master Johannes illuminated for the goldsmiths' guild of Vác a manuscript containing texts of the Mass and religious songs. He must certainly also have illuminated manuscripts for his bishop, but none has survived; his art is thus known to posterity only from the ceremonial book prepared for the goldsmiths' guild of Vác (Budapest, OSZK Clmae 377). On the ornate title-page, the patron of goldsmiths, St Eloi, is standing in the initial with a golden goblet in his left hand, and a splendid large ring on his right. By his side are seen goldsmiths' tools, an anvil and a hammer, painted in a realistic style. In the border decoration the miniaturist used only a few leaf motifs; these are painted more stiffly, wherein he followed the pattern of the less delicate ornamentation of goldsmiths, as also in the unusual winding, interwoven lines of the foliated scroll. This manner of decoration was not unique in Hungary. In the border ornamentation of the plainer Esztergom Breviary prepared in 1421 (Vienna, National Library Cod. lat. 1829), leaves of heavier form wind around the stalks in the scroll; though they are the work of a less outstanding master, they display an affinity to the ornamental design of Master Johannes. It is typical of his art that in contrast to the slightly solemn and conventional representation of the saint, the painting of the calligraphic initials inserted into the text and among the notes is much more informal. Here he painted in dilute colours heads of men and women with individual, characteristic traits, which may be taken for portraits (including, perhaps, a self-portrait); there is sometimes a slight distortion of the features, as in a caricature (Figs. 14a and b).

In the twenties and thirties of the 15th century an important workshop of miniaturists was active for sixteen years (1423–1439) at the court of Georgius Pálóczy, Archbishop of Esztergom, who fought against the increasingly widespread Hussite movement not only with words but also with arms. He is the only book-lover from the entourage of King Sigismund whose illuminated manuscripts have survived. Three of his books for ecclesiastical purposes have come down to posterity, all of them lavishly illuminated, each painted by a different miniaturist. Most likely several artists worked at his court. In all probability it was King Matthias's faithless archbishop, Johannes Beckensloer, who took with him an ornate breviary of Pálóczy's to Salzburg (Salzburg, Studienbibliothek V. I. E. 60) when he exchanged the archbishopric of Esztergom for that of Salzburg. A missal of Pálóczy may be found in the National Széchényi Library in Budapest (Clmae 359), while a large, richly illuminated antiphonary is in the possession of the Esztergom Cathedral Library.

The Missal of Pálóczy which is in Budapest is a typical and arresting piece of Hungarian miniature painting. The Canon has been cut out (presumably it represented Christ on the Cross), but ten border decorations and eight initials bear testimony to the work of an important master. In the initials the miniaturist painted scenes from the life

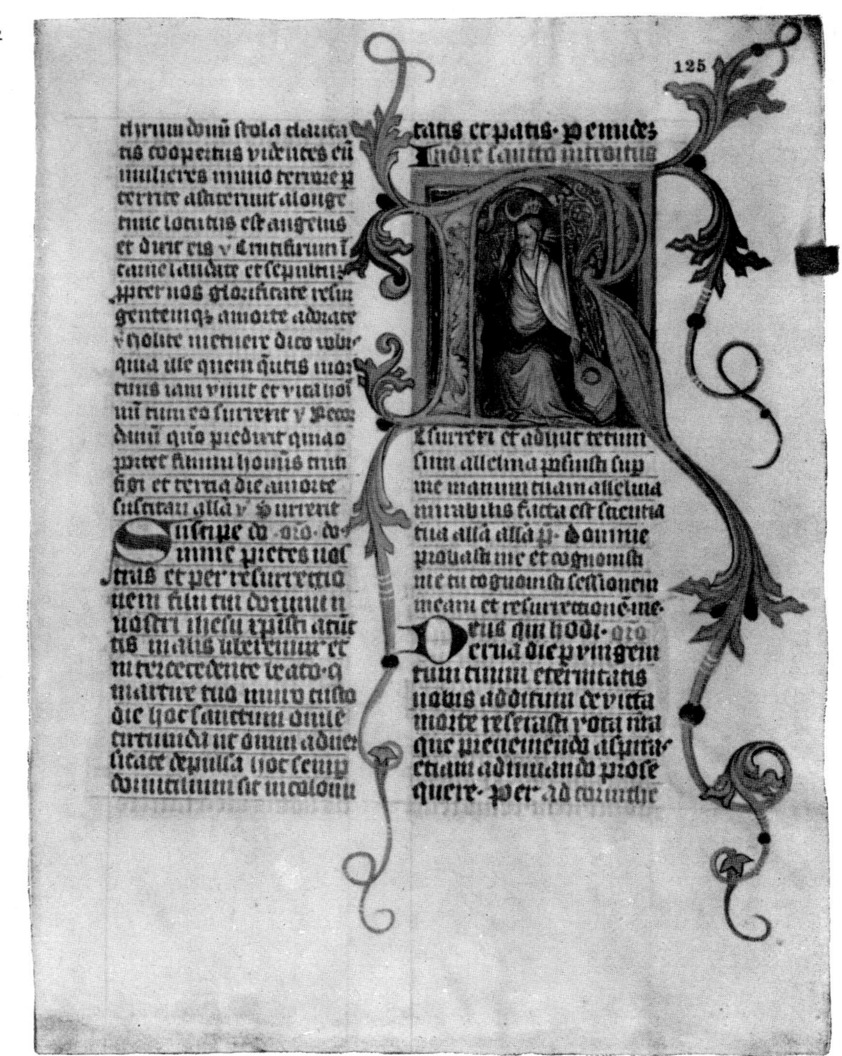

22

of Christ, telling the story attractively in colourful compositions with many figures. His figures, in conformity with Hungarian taste, are not in the elongated, nervous manner of the Gothic, but are slightly clumsy and stocky (Plate XVII; Figs. 15–20). A definite relationship in the decoration is noticeable between the Pálóczy Missal of Budapest and his Antiphonary of Esztergom: if the two manuscripts were illuminated by two different miniaturists, both volumes are obviously products of the same workshop. The Antiphonary was intended to be a more ornate work than the Missal of Budapest. The former consists of two volumes the first of which was left without illumination. The second volume is mutilated and incomplete. Owing to its damaged condition it contains far fewer decorations than does the Missal; but the execution is more magnificent, and the size more impressive.

The two manuscripts resemble each other especially in the design of the border decorations, although also in the border decorations of Gothic foliated scroll illuminating the Antiphonary there may be found realistic flowers and animals—squirrels, apes and owls. In the colouring of the decorations there is in general a difference between the two manuscripts. Moreover, in contrast to the rich compositions with many figures in the small initials of the Missal, in the only figured initial of the Antiphonary the miniaturist painted a calm, dignified Virgin of distinguished carriage, with the Child on her arm (Plate XVIII).

At the time when Thomas de Coloswar painted his altarpiece of Garamszentbenedek, two excellent miniaturists were active in the mining towns of Northern Hungary. One was the anonymous Master of Körmöcbánya who illuminated the minute-book of the town of Körmöcbánya in 1426, before the altar of Garamszentbenedek was finished. This minute-book is still in the town archives. The Anonymous Master painted two full-page miniatures in the volume: a Crucifixion and a picture of the Day of Judgment. The latter would be a suitable composition even for a monumental fresco. On the evidence of these two miniatures the Master of Körmöcbánya must have painted panels too. This is suggested also by the plainer, unpretentious border decorations: the miniaturist was not interested in painting more elaborate border ornamentation. Two more works of this master are known: a Breviary (Vienna, National Library Cod. 4812) and the magnificently executed Missal of Pozsony (Budapest, OSZK Clmae 218). The Canon of this Missal has also been cut out, but 14 folios have frames of richly foliated, floral design.

In seven large initials there are also representations on the following themes: King David (fol. 9; Plate XIX); the Nativity (fol. 20v; Fig. 21); Christ on the Mount of Olives (fol. 120; Fig. 23); Christ Triumphant (fol. 125; Fig. 22); an old man (fol. 220); the Tongues of Fire or the Pentecost (fol. 128); and a blond woman at prayer (the Virgin?) (fol. 233). In the smaller initials the miniaturist painted scenes with several figures, as if composing panels: for instance in the initial of the Canon in the Missal, where Christ is represented praying on the Mount of Olives.

The art of the Master of Körmöcbánya and that of Thomas de Coloswar show many kindred features, though the minute-book of Körmöcbánya was painted a year before the altarpiece of Garamszentbenedek. That the two artists came from related circles may be recognized in the similar painting of faces and folds of garments, particularly in the figure of Christ praying on the Mount of Olives. Relationship of style is shown primarily in the use of similar forms: both in the triptych of Thomas de Coloswar and in the works of the Master of Körmöcbánya, though these are most naive in conception, there is manifested that expressive power which they derived from

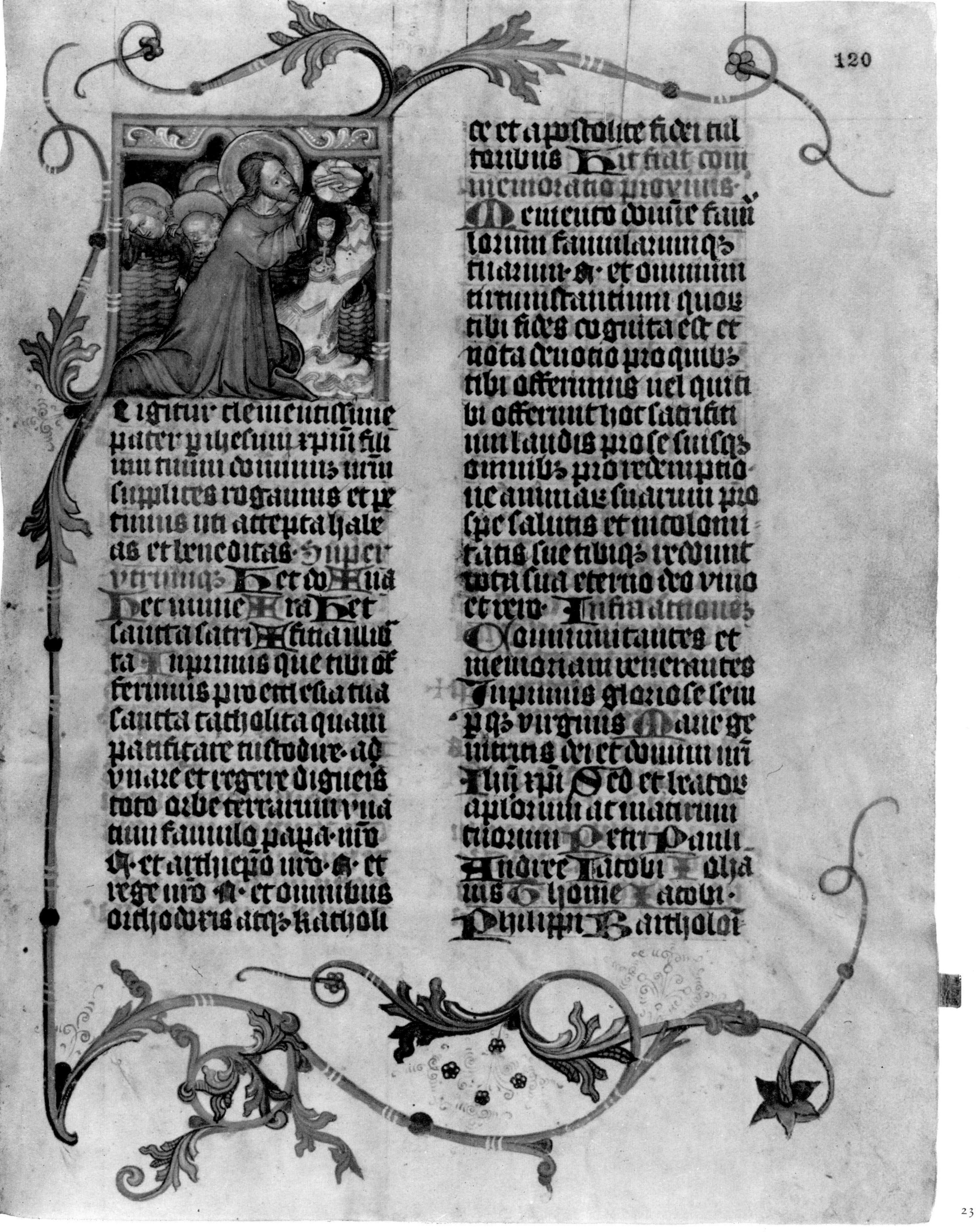

Te igitur clementissime
pater per ihesum christum filium
tuum dominum nostrum
supplices rogamus et pe-
timus uti accepta habe-
as et benedicas. Super
utrumque. Hec dona hec
munera hec
sancta sacrificia illiba-
ta. In primis que tibi offerimus pro ecclesia tua
sancta catholica quam
pacificare custodire adu-
nare et regere digneris
toto orbe terrarum una
cum famulo tuo papa nostro
N. et antistite nostro N. et
rege nostro N. et omnibus
orthodoxis atque catholi-

ce et apostolice fidei cultoribus. Hic fiat com-
memoratio pro vivis.
Memento domine famu-
lorum famularumque
tuarum N. et omnium
circumstantium quorum
tibi fides cognita est et
nota devotio pro quibus
tibi offerimus uel qui tibi offerunt hoc sacrificium laudis pro se suisque
omnibus pro redemptio-
ne animarum suarum pro
spe salutis et incolumi-
tatis sue tibique reddunt
uota sua eterno deo uiuo
et vero. Infra actionem.
Communicantes et
memoriam venerantes
In primis gloriose sem-
per virginis Marie ge-
nitricis dei et domini nostri
Ihesu christi. Sed et beatorum
apostolorum ac martirum
tuorum Petri Pauli
Andree Iacobi Iohan-
nis Thome Iacobi
Philippi Bartholomei

the peculiarities of their native country. Indeed, the works of the Master of Körmöcbánya display similarity also with other products of Hungarian painting of the time. For example, in the museum of Košice there is a picture from the early 15th century representing the Raising of Lazarus. Here the thin, bearded faces and the elongated figures show such a close resemblance to the figures in the miniatures of the Master of Körmöcbánya as to raise the question whether the miniatures and the panels were not painted by the same hand. The Master of Körmöcbánya plays an important role not only in the history of Hungarian miniature art, but in the whole of early Hungarian art.

The other excellent miniaturist of Northern Hungary painted in 1432 the minute-book of the town of Selmecbánya (Budapest, Hungarian National Museum, Historical Department No. 61.54c). Like that of Körmöcbánya, this minute-book also contains a full-page miniature of the Crucifixion (Plate XXI). The painter, as stated in the older literature on the subject and in a badly worn inscription on the last page, folio 192, was Valentinus Gobil of Selmec. Compared to the Late Gothic forms of the Master of Körmöcbánya, his art is calmer, more harmonious, gentle and lyrical, in keeping with Italian taste.

In the only miniature of a paper manuscript from Kassa in Northern Hungary (Alba Iulia, Batthyanaeum R. II. 7), representing Christ in the company of scholars and priests, there is a similarity of artistic conception. On the other hand, a magnificent large miniature representing Calvary, torn out of another manuscript from Northern Hungary, is related to the art of the Master of Körmöcbánya (Budapest, Museum of Fine Arts; Plate XX). Whereas the Calvary of the Selmecbánya minute-book is quiet and without deep emotion, here the theme is represented with Late Gothic realism. Not resignation to divine destiny nor faith in resurrection is here expressed; in the suffering figure of Christ there is human emotion, and particularly in the passionate representation of the Virgin, in her maternal grief there is drama without pathos. Here may be seen the striving of the Late Gothic art to convey human feelings, pain and tragedy through scenes from the New Testament representing the life of Christ. Such works were painted by artists who lived among the people; and perhaps we shall not be mistaken if in such portrayals of the sufferings of Christ and in numerous other similar representations of biblical scenes in the paintings and sculptures of Northern Hungary we find echoes of the growing revolutionary movement of the persecuted Hussites.

In its profound portrayal of human woe and suffering this Late Gothic realism, as it is called, shows progressive tendencies; later, however, it was gradually to lose ground in Hungarian miniature painting as Renaissance art came to dominate. In Northern Hungary, where Gothic trends persisted longest, the Renaissance appeared first in endeavours to emphasize beauty and harmony and decorative ornamental forms. This stage is graphically illustrated in the initial decorated with foliated scroll on a leaf from another manuscript of Northern Hungary (Budapest, Museum of Fine Arts); the initial is still Gothic, but Martha is now represented as a high-born, graceful, coquettish lady, like the beautiful female saints seen also on triptychs, who are clad in attire worn by the aristocracy of the age, in sharp contrast to the popular representations of indigent saints previously prevalent in panel painting and in miniature art (Plate XXII).

By the middle of the 15th century humanism was becoming ever stronger among the ruling classes of Hungary. This meant a new time of great progress, but also a stiffening of resistance on the part of the ruling classes against the Hussites and the peasant revolts. During the regency of Johannes Hunyadi (1446–1452), Johannes Vitéz, Bishop of Nyitra (now Nitra, Czechoslovakia), then of Nagyvárad (now Oradea, Rumania), finally Archbishop of Esztergom—earlier, in his young years, clerk of the chancellery at Sigismund's court—became a strong adherent of the humanism spreading from

24

25

Italy. A great lover of books, Vitéz evinced particular interest in classical Latin authors, as did later also his nephew, Johannes Csezmicei, better known as Janus Pannonius, the illustrious Hungarian humanist poet, who had been educated in Italy. The circle of his friends included German scholars. Regiomontanus, who dedicated his work entitled *Canones* to King Matthias (Budapest, OSZK Clmae 412) spent some time at the court of Johannes Vitéz. The manuscript Canones was undoubtedly copied in Hungary, and one of its pages (fol. 3) was decorated with the Gothic illumination still generally employed at the time. One of the earliest pieces of Johannes Vitéz's collection, the Victorinus Manuscript, which was transferred to the library of Matthias after the death of Vitéz (Budapest, OSZK Clmae 370; Fig. 26), had been made in Hungary.

In this Corvina manuscript of the work of Victorinus the illumination was also still executed in the Gothic style, but the floral and animal motifs in the Gothic scroll ornaments, the birds shown so realistically among the bright flowers, point to a Renaissance conception. The endeavour to represent phenomena of nature in a realistic manner persisted in Hungarian miniature painting, particularly in the treatment of sacred themes, and developed side by side with Renaissance culture. For instance, in the Gothic foliated scrolls forming the border decoration on two pages of a Missal (Esztergom, FK Mss. I. 20) prepared in the diocese of Esztergom about 1480 for a church in Pozsony, there are several flowers painted in a realistic manner (Plate XXIII, Fig. 27). In a Breviary from 1450 (Budapest, OSZK Clmae 409) there is a striking example of stylized foliated scroll ornament being applied in an individual manner, and with a taste perhaps derived from folk motifs. This volume shows a close relationship to the Antiphonary of Franciscus Futaki dated 1463, illuminated with simplified motifs; the latter manuscript is in the Seraglio Library of Istanbul.

Splendid Hungarian works of this age are to be found in other countries, including a gradual of Johannes Han, canon of Pozsony (Bratislava, Capitular Library), and the fragments of another gradual of his (Bratislava, Town Archives), both of which were illuminated with unusual abundance of ornamentation by an excellent miniaturist in 1487. In addition to rich border decorations of foliated scrolls with stylized Gothic flowers and fine miniatures on sacred themes, the calligraphic initials in the text contain interesting representations of figures from the people—for instance, a peasant carrying a big sack on his back. The same outstanding miniaturist is considered to have

26

executed the later 15th-century decoration in the illuminated Missal of Henry, parish priest of Csukárd, painted in 1377 (Alba Iulia, Batthyanaeum R. II. 134), and also the less elaborate border decorations of a Missal of Pozsony prepared in the year 1488 (Budapest, OSZK Clmae 219). There are names inscribed among the decorations in the Missal of Alba Iulia, and the miniaturist of Johannes Han has been identified as Matthias Prenner.

Noteworthy artistic work is to be found in two incunabula illuminated in medieval Hungary, now preserved in other countries. One is Guido de Baysio's incunabulum, from Lőcse (now Levoča, Czechoslovakia), which was printed about 1473 at Strassburg by Mentelin (Alba Iulia, Batthyanaeum Inc. V. 6). In a large miniature on the title-page the pope may be seen in the company of cardinals and bishops. The other incunabulum, Johannes Petrus de Ferraris's work, the *Completio moderne iudicialis practice*, was also printed in the year of 1473, at Venice (Bardejov, Šariš Museum). It is assumed that the title-page was illuminated by an artist of Bártfa in the 1470s; it is lavishly decorated with the rich coils of a splendid foliated scroll and with a large miniature, in the centre of which may be seen the female symbol of Justice in the company of the pope and a king with a long beard; in front of them, small by comparison, is a young peasant hoeing potatoes. There has also survived, in the incunabulum, a fine unfinished sketch by a scribe of a large miniature.

Recent research has identified the works of two anonymous miniaturists who illustrated incunabula and were active at the end of the 15th century and the beginning of the 16th. At Besztercebánya and Bártfa (now Banská Bistrica, resp. Bardejov, Czechoslovakia), Balthasar Blutfogel, a Silesian by birth and educated at Cracow, decorated, among other volumes, some manuscripts and incunabula from his own collection, which comprised, so far as is known at present, twenty-two pieces; the ornamentation consisted of simple Gothic foliated scroll ornament and initials, without any figural composition. Of the volumes illuminated by Blutfogel himself eight are in the Historical Department of the Hungarian National Museum, one in the Archiepiscopal Library of Eger, and one in the State Library at Košice (RMK 197). The decorations of a small German prayer book are also attributed to him (Budapest, EK Cod. Germ. 2. 8°).

A much more important artist than Balthasar Blutfogel was the illustrator of Franciscus Gratianus's incunabulum, the *Decretum*, printed in Venice in 1474 and preserved at Szepeshely (now Spišská Kapitula, Czechoslovakia) in the Capitular Library of Szepes. Be-

tam uos cum in mundo. Et hij
in mundo sunt et ego ad te
venio. Offr. Ascendit deus i
iubilacione et dns in voce tube
alla. Secr. Sacrificium tibi
dne pro filij tui supplices nunc
venerabili ascensione defe
rimus presta qs ut nos per
ipsum hijs commerciis sacro
sanctis ad celestia consurgamus.
Qui tecum. Com. Pr cum es
sem cum eis ego seruabam eos quos
dedisti michi alla nunc ad te ve
nio non rogo ut tollas eos de mun
do sed ut serues eos a malo alla
alla. Compl. Tribue qs
dne ut per hec sacramenta que
sumpsimus illuc tendat
christiane deuocionis affectus
quo tecum est nra substancia
ihs xps dns nr. Qui tecum.
In die ascensionis dni ad
aspersione aque bndicte. Vidi
aquam. V. Dne apud te est fons
vite. Et in lumine tuo videbimus
Omnips sempit ds. lumen.
Due deus deduc nos ad
societatem celestium gaudiorum
ut gra tui spus renatus reg
num tuum facias introire atque
ab eo perueniat humilitas gre

gis quo precessit celsitudo pa
storis. Per eundem. Ad processio
nem. R. iiii. Ite in orbem. V. As
cendens xps in altum alla. R. Cap
tiuam duxit captiuitatem alla.
Tribue qs ops ds.
ceus ut munere festi
uitatis hodierne illuc filio
rum tuorum dirigatur in
tencio quo in tuo unigenito te
cum est substancia nra ihs xps
dns nr. Qui tecum. In resurrec
tione. Salue festa. ympnus.
Ihu nra redempcio. V. Ascendit
deus in iubilacione alla. Et dns
in voce tube alleluia. Oracio.
Deus qui nos redemcionis
dnice et ascensionis e
letabunda sollempnia cele
brare fecisti da famulis tuis
ut venientis celsius gratiam
purificatis mentibus suscipe
mereamur. Per. Ad magnam missam.

Viri ga
lilei quid
admirami
ni aspi
cientes
in celum
alla
que ad

tween 1474 and 1479 he illuminated this book with numerous remarkable miniatures, in which he mingled Gothic ornamentation with realistic flowers, signing his work with evident self-assurance: *Istum librum illuminavit Vincentius Roder Czinteke*. The miniatures on worldly themes, pointing to the influence of contemporary engravings, illustrate legal cases with representations of the life of the town-dwellers at the close of the 15th century. In one of the larger miniatures, for example, we see a man with his legs in the stocks; and the pictures of an affianced couple, two citizens conversing, a boy being adopted illuminate social history. Besides miniatures, Czinteke painted initials which are individual in conception; handsome flowers, realistically painted, are entwined with the ornamental Gothic foliated scrolls.

The use of Gothic foliated scrolls as border decoration were still practised in Hungarian provincial miniature art of the 16th century. While the painting of realistic animal motifs and flowers became more frequent, under the influence of the court of King Matthias at Buda Gothic foliated scroll ornament was to be ingeniously mingled with the brilliance and richness of Renaissance decorative elements. A small Breviary of modest execution (Budapest, OSZK Clmae 343) owned by Stephanus Nagylaki, canon of Bács and Fehérvár, may be mentioned as an example. This manuscript was made in the year 1489; in the border decoration of the title-page Gothic foliated scrolls are combined with ornamental motifs in the Renaissance taste such as were painted by the artists in the miniature workshop of Matthias Corvinus. Other border decorations follow Gothic traditions, but the restlessly winding foliated scrolls are enlivened by realistic motifs of flowers and also coloured birds, including an occasional owl; we even see a hunter aiming his arrow at a small bird (Fig. 34).

RENAISSANCE MINIATURE ART

Matthias Corvinus, the great Hungarian Renaissance sovereign (1458–1490), ascended the throne as a young man. Having acquired wide humanist learning, he founded a magnificent library, the Bibliotheca Corviniana. Ornate works of Italian humanists were brought to Hungary for prelates and nobles, but especially for the court of Buda. Already in the first half of Matthias's reign, long before his marriage to Beatrice of Aragon, daughter of the king of Naples, in 1476, there was at the court a busy workshop for painting the letters patent of the royal chancellery as well as a workshop of copyists, scribes and miniaturists. There is documentary evidence that Blandius, a humanist miniaturist of Matthias, was working at Buda in 1471, in which year he was sent by the king to Italy for the purchase of books.

Already in the seventies, despite Late Gothic tendencies in Hungary, the miniaturists' workshop of Buda already followed the spirit and artistic conceptions of Italian Renaissance miniature art. Although as early as the sixties many manuscripts were brought to Buda from Florence where they had been decorated by Florentine miniaturists in the humanist style, particularly those made in the workshop of the bookseller Vespasiano da Bisticci, we do not know of a single work produced in Buda which is decorated with intertwined white foliated scrolls in the style of Florentine manuscripts. In the seventies, one of King Matthias's miniaturists—perhaps Blandius—illuminated works which had been copied at Buda and also several manuscripts which had been brought in an unadorned state from Italy; adopting with good taste the motifs of Florentine Renaissance miniature art, he applied modest foliated, floral decoration. An example is the title-page of the Corvina manuscript *Compendium grammaticae* by Georgius Trapezuntius (Budapest, OSZK Clmae 428), where the artist painted the king's arms in the middle of the lower margin and on either side placed an enchanting, winged *putto* (Fig. 28). Around 1480, when the king's miniature workshop had come to greater maturity, we know from available records that Francesco di Lorenzo Roselli was active in Buda, and also, somewhat later, the excellent Ferraran painter, Ercole de' Roberti. Several

28

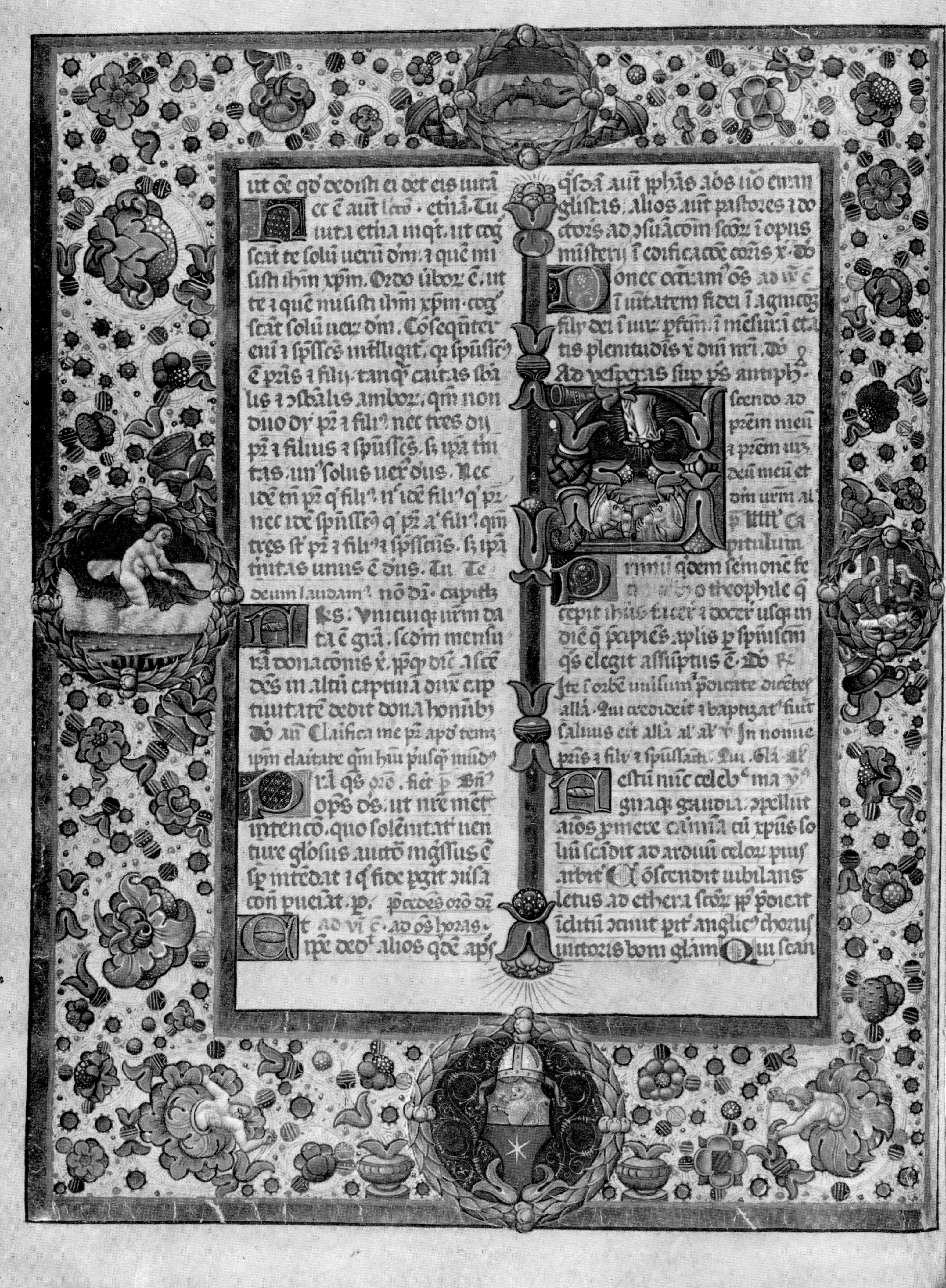

artists are known to have come from Italy and to have worked in the court miniature workshop of King Matthias, where they illuminated not only manuscripts for the King and for nobles of the Hungarian aristocracy, but also liturgical volumes for prelates. Most of the highly ornate manuscripts which have survived from the Buda workshop of Matthias are now by a strange chance the treasures of libraries and collections in other countries. Apart from the previously mentioned simple and earlier illuminated Corvina manuscripts, only one sumptuously decorated manuscript of Buda workmanship is to be found in Hungary, namely Trapezuntius's *Rhetorica* (Budapest, OSZK Clmae 281). There are, however, several outstanding works which were illuminated at the court of Buda for the King's prelates.

Outstanding artists from other countries, whose names have come down to us, are known to have been active at King Matthias's workshop, together with their Hungarian pupils. For instance, Francesco di Kastello Ithallico probably worked at Buda from the late seventies, and the eminent Giovanni Antonio Cattaneo de Mediolano who arrived in Buda in 1482, also the important Dalmatian scholar and diplomat, Felice Petanzio Ragusino (Felix Petancius Ragusinus), who, according to recent Croatian research, reached Buda in 1487 and became the head of the workshop there. These masters and their Hungarian pupils, by blending the diverse motifs and elements of local Italian schools, evolved the ornamental style peculiar to the workshop of Buda and perhaps also to that of Visegrád, thus lending a special local character not only to decorative motifs, but also to types of faces and figures.

At the workshop each miniaturist produced work of the quality corresponding to his talents, and these artists exerted mutual influence on one another. It may also be presumed that the illumination of a manuscript in the workshop was not done throughout by the same miniaturist; the highly elaborate pages of richly ornamented manuscripts may each have been illuminated by a different miniaturist. It is even possible that sometimes the decorative border motifs on a page were painted by one miniaturist, while the figures in the medallions inserted among the motifs, or the initials in the text were the work of another hand.

It will be one of the tasks of future historians of art to study the works produced by the miniature workshop of Matthias and later by that of the King Wladislas II with these possibilities in mind.

During its existence of several decades the products of the court

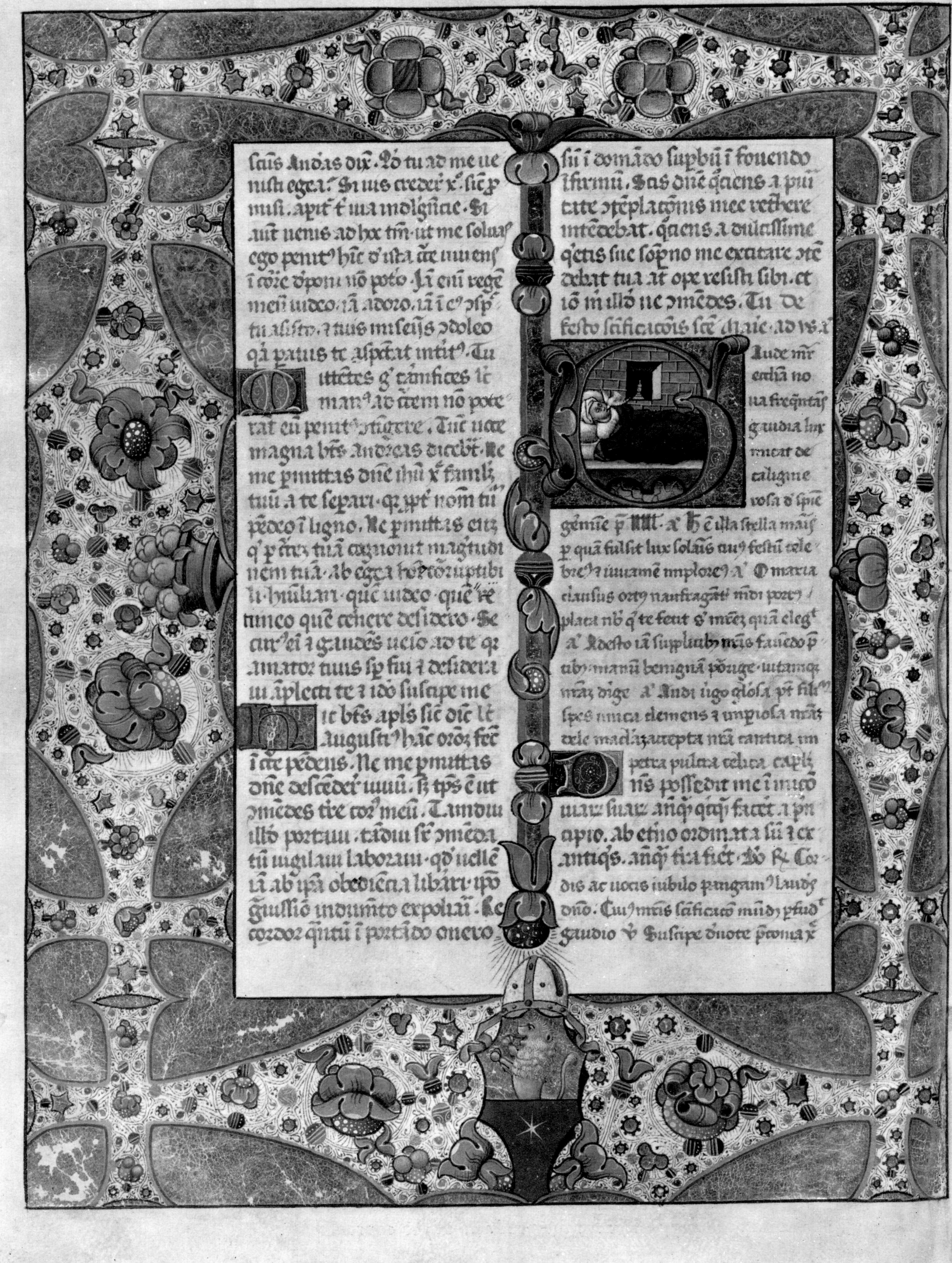

miniaturists' workshop show unmistakable progress, especially in an increasing wealth of decorative motifs. This advance was greatly influenced by increasing acquaintance with the profusion of ornamental elements in manuscripts made in the artistic circle of Attavante which were arriving from Italy, chiefly from Florence, and by familiarity with the motifs used to decorate Italian majolica.

In general, the masters of the workshop strove with an extraordinary sense of beauty to give expression to Renaissance splendour and wealth, but the realistic representation of human emotions, which had prevailed earlier in Hungarian miniature painting, was abandoned. Biblical scenes and figured compositions were assigned a subordinate role in the decorative scheme, which sought to create a gorgeous and spectacular effect. Strong stress, however, is laid on the realistic details of ornamentation. The border-frame decorations consist of splendid flowers and motifs of antique acanthus leaves; and in contrast to the religious themes of sacred art, amidst a luxurious abundance of pearls, precious stones, golden vases interspersed with lances, armour, shields and helmets there appear, inspired by the new art of the Renaissance as a reflection of classical antiquity, typical motifs of the ancient, pagan world and mythology: Tritons, sirens and centaurs, sometimes even antique deities.

In other cases religious compositions and biblical themes are presented in a profane setting: the life of a Christian saint is painted in a worldly, often aristocratic environment. Moreover, in the compositions with figures in the Corvina manuscripts illuminated at the King's miniature workshop in Buda, one may notice representations which not only express the artistic conception of the age but also reveal the miniaturist's emotions. Striking examples, to mention only a few, are to be seen in the series of biblical compositions painted by Francesco di Kastello in the lavishly decorated manuscript of Dominicus Kálmáncsehi, Provost of Székesfehérvár (1474–1495), and in his Breviary (Budapest, OSZK Clmae 446). The artist represented in a very curious manner the theme of the Nativity, and especially the setting out and the meeting of the Three Magi. They are painted in contemporary dress as valiant, martial nobles of the Renaissance (fol. 100); moreover, unlike the accepted iconography of the theme of the Three Magi, the scenes of their story, which is told with an arresting gift for narrative detail, are depicted in medallions which are fitted in a remarkably individual manner into the four corners of the parchment. The so-called "insipient", denying the teachings of Christ, is painted as a court fool (fol. 23). In a marginal miniature,

32

Dominicus Kálmáncsehi is painted kneeling, like a Renaissance donor, before the Virgin and Child (fol. 308; Plate XXX). The lower decoration on the same page is a brilliant worldly scene depicting a wild-boar hunt, the noble pastime which was a favourite theme of the age; it is a more simple variety of the theme painted by the Limbourg brothers. In another manuscript of Dominicus Kálmáncsehi, in his Missal (Zagreb, Archiepiscopal Library MR 355), an extremely interesting and rare motif is found in the scene of Calvary: besides representing a brutal crowd and a king, the artist has painted in the foreground the figure of a Renaissance court jester (Fig. 32).

Francesco di Kastello Ithallico is the first important miniaturist of the court of King Matthias who is known to posterity not only by name but also by a magnificent, authentically signed work, namely the Breviary of Dominicus Kálmáncsehi of which we have already spoken. Formerly in possession of the Benedictine monastery of

Lambach, it was transferred to the National Széchényi Library in the 1930s. This manuscript of the Buda workshop is remarkable not only for the extraordinary splendour of its illumination, but also because on two decorated pages the master boldly signed his name, which is unusual in miniature art. In a winding band at the inner edge of folio 215 "Opus Francisci de Kastello Ithallico de Mediolano" may be read in capital letters (Plate XXVIII), and again on folio 428 "francisce de castello italico". Thus among the miniaturists of the workshop of Buda, Francesco di Kastello is the first of whom it can be said that an authentic work by his hand is known to posterity.

As a rule only the title-page or the last page of Corvina manuscripts was illuminated at the workshop of Buda. The Corvina Breviary preserved in the Vatican Library is perhaps the only exception. The Kálmáncsehi Breviary, which is in Budapest, is richly illuminated with miniatures and figured initials. This manuscript has the remarkable feature that the influence exerted by the respective styles of different Italian local schools may be traced in the decorations of various pages. Thus brilliant elaborate floral decorations accompanied by Florentine beads, garlands and vases may be observed on some pages, and Ferraran ornamental motifs on others. Lombardian patterns were also favourite decorative elements, but in the art of Francesco di Kastello Ithallico, beside the use of Lombardian ornamental forms, Ferraran motifs were allowed to dominate so noticeably as to suggest that the artist may have stayed at Ferrara for a considerable period of time. At all events it may be taken for granted that Francesco di Kastello came to Buda from Ferrara, as did later, in 1482, another excellent miniaturist of King Matthias, Giovanni Antonio Cattaneo de Mediolano.

The border decorations of the Kálmáncsehi Breviary of Budapest are so exceedingly varied that they can hardly be taken throughout for the work of one and the same artist. In some places archaizing motifs occur in the ornamentation. Gothic influence is obvious in the painting of grotesque monsters, not encountered in any other volume produced by the workshop of Buda. In other places the workmanship is slightly clumsy, even rough—particularly in the border decorations—compared to the art of other eminent masters of King Matthias. At the same time the Kálmáncsehi Breviary contains miniatures painted with extraordinary, masterly lightness of touch, such as the superlatively beautiful hunting motifs inspired by foreign models. The types of faces are also softer and more delicate than in other works produced at Buda (Plates XXIV–XXXI; Figs. 29–31).

A letters patent made by the master of the Kálmáncsehi Breviary at the court of Buda in 1481 is also known to posterity. Hence it is clear that Francesco di Kastello Ithallico also painted letters patent at the chancellery for Matthias. How far he cooperated in the illumination of Corvina manuscripts in Hungary is a question which cannot yet be definitely answered. But his influence and contribution may certainly be seen in later works from Buda, for instance in the Zagreb Missal of Kálmáncsehi. His hand may also be seen in another manuscript of Dominicus Kálmáncsehi, prepared in 1492, that is to say in the reign of Wladislas II (1490–1516), at present in the National Library in Paris. His influence gradually began to wane in the late eighties, although some of his peculiar flower motifs may be found, greatly enlarged, in the art of one of the miniaturists employed by Osvaldus Thuz, Bishop of Zagreb (who died in 1499). Several liturgical manuscripts were made for Dominicus Kálmáncsehi at the miniaturist workshop of King Matthias. One of these manuscripts, a Missal, shown by an inscription to have been made in 1481, is in America after having been in the Liechtenstein Collection first in Vienna, then in Vaduz.

33

Kálmáncsehi's Prayer Book, formerly in a private collection in London, is now in Paris (Bibl. Nat. Nouv. acqu. lat. 3119). This manuscript was prepared in 1492, that is in the reign of the Hungarian King Wladislas II. Upon closer study it furnishes a remarkable picture of the Corvina workshop of Buda and the development of its artistic style, for we find here a blending of the different decorative elements used in the Buda workshop. The volume is the work of several hands, and in its thirty-seven border decorations the contributions of four or five miniaturists may be distinguished. The whole manuscript creates the impression that at the wish of Provost Kálmáncsehi the miniaturists may have imitated the illumination of some richly decorated pages of Corvina manuscripts. For instance, the central part of a mythological battle on folio 1v in the Philostratus Corvina Manuscript at Budapest (Budapest, OSZK Clmae 417) is to be found copied on folio 124v of the Prayer Book.

One might almost think that the manuscript had been a highly ornate, magnificent pattern book for miniaturists. Among the masters who contributed to the illumination of this volume there may be recognized on several pages the characteristically individual work of Francesco di Kastello Ithallico, with his sometimes slightly heavy lines but varied and brightly coloured ornamentation. But although he may be assumed to have painted some pages in this manuscript written in 1492, the rest of the decorations, perhaps owing to his departure or death, were painted by other miniaturists of Buda after Corvina manuscripts brought from abroad, for instance after works by Attavante and Cherico which have been lost.

These masters also made use of the border decorations of eminent Buda miniaturists, for example the magnificent decorations of the Aristotle Corvina incunabulum in five volumes, at present in Paris (Bibl. Nat. Inc. Vélins 478), and the Cassianus Corvina Manuscript, also in Paris (Bibl. Nat. Ms. lat. 2129). On one page of the Prayer Book the attention is caught by the work of an outstanding but quite unknown artist (fol. 46v) who must surely have been trained in Italy, and whose gentle, lyrical motifs brought to Buda a new quality of sweetness, contrasting with the severe, firm lines of the faces characteristic of the Corvina workshop.

In the eighties the most outstanding personality at King Matthias's miniature workshop was Giovanni Antonio Cattaneo de Mediolano, a Dominican monk, who asked for leave of absence from the Dominican monastery of Ferrara, Santa Maria degli Angeli, in February 1482 that he might travel to Hungary, where he arrived in June of the same year. On the evidence of contemporary records, he worked at the court also in the years 1495 and 1498 as the miniaturist of Wladislas II. In a Corvina Gradual (Budapest, OSZK Clmae 424) made in France, his art may be studied in a splendid miniature, signed with a monogram. With deep, personal emotion the miniature portrays the entry of the Jews into the Promised Land. In the background the master painted a view of Visegrád, and in the foreground there is the group of marching figures, including Matthias's miniaturists, among whom the artist set his self-portrait. The slender figures and the faces of delicate individuality make his work very different from the average products of the royal workshop of miniaturists. He was an artist of extraordinary skill. On the ground of the high qualities of this miniature, the illumination of the Averulinus Corvina Manuscript preserved at the Marciana Library in Venice and the illumination of some pages of the Vatican Corvina Breviary may also be attributed to him.

According to several recently stated views Giovanni Cattaneo cannot be regarded as an illuminator of manuscripts, because in the yearly account for 1495 of Wladislas II he is called "miniaturist of royal books" *(librorum regiorum)*. We cannot accept the interpretation that the word "miniator" does not denote "illuminator". Apart from the large figured initial, the other miniatures of the Gradual were

34

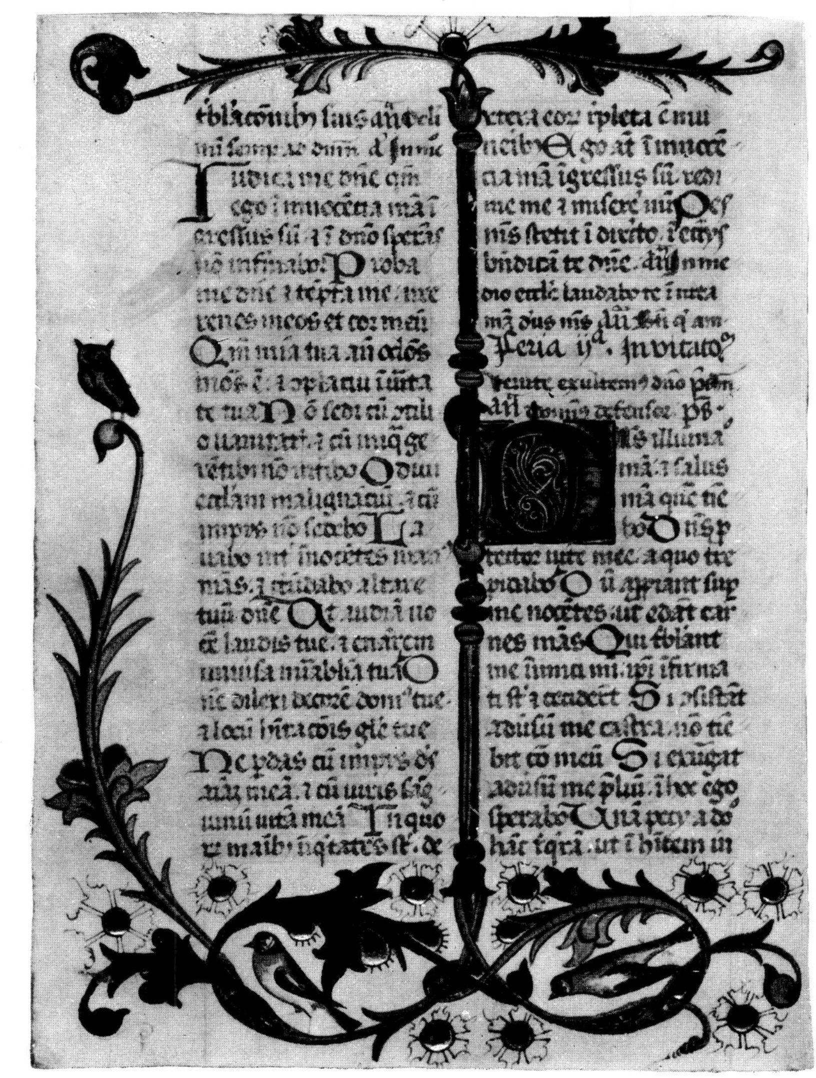

painted in an excellent French workshop under Flemish influence, as already pointed out in an earlier volume discussing the Library of Matthias Corvinus.* The argument that the whole of the Gradual was produced in Hungary at a Franciscan scriptorium for some Franciscan monastery, is also not convincing, since no artistic allusion can be found in the manuscript to the cult of St Francis, St Clara, or St Elizabeth of Hungary. Nor can one accept as satisfactory proof the assertion that a hooded mendicant friar in the miniatures is to be identified as a Franciscan, and that a clearly Dominican priest is to be recognized as a monk belonging to the order of St Paul. Also erroneous and equally untenable is the assumption that the large initial was painted at the Corvina workshop of Buda by a Lombardian or Milanese master, while the rest of the miniatures were painted by some "less gifted miniaturist" of the Buda workshop after Franco-Flemish patterns.

* Berkovits, Ilona: *Illuminated Manuscripts from the Library of Matthias Corvinus.* Budapest, 1964.

In Buda at this time there were not only a copyist and a miniaturist workshop active at the court of King Matthias, but a special bookbinder's workshop had also been set up, where the volumes destined for the library of the Hungarian Renaissance monarch were bound in covers of rare beauty and typical form. These bindings have the remarkable feature that even the gilt edge of the parchment leaves of the manuscript is often decorated with vividly coloured motifs and floral patterns. The Renaissance love of brilliance and splendour and its fondness for exuberant decoration were manifested in every field of applied art. The pictures painted by great Renaissance artists had always to be set in golden frames adorned with rich floral ornamentation and coloured garlands. Similarly, the richness of the bindings made at Buda for Corvina manuscripts was frequently enhanced by abundantly decorating the gilt edge of the parchment leaves of a manuscript with brightly coloured motifs. These decorations are often of a high artistic standard; for instance, the exceedingly beautiful gilt edge (Plate XXXV) of the Cyprianus Corvina Manuscript, recently purchased in London (Budapest, OSZK Clmae 529), indicates that in some cases the coloured ornamentation of the gilt edge was painted by Matthias's miniaturists at the workshop of Buda.

Although not many of the Corvina manuscripts produced in Buda are at present to be found in Hungary, they include, besides the Kálmáncsehi Breviary, the lavishly decorated Pontifical illuminated for Johannes Filipecz, Bishop of Nagyvárad (1476–1490), and the Psalter of Urbanus Dóczi de Nagylucse, Bishop of Eger (1487–1492). In the Pontifical of Johannes Filipecz (Esztergom, FK Ms. 26), besides the minor initials and miniatures representing clerical and episcopal rituals, the elaborate border decoration of the manuscript's title-page (Plate XXXII) and its numerous richly ornamented pages bear testimony to the artist's extremely refined taste; the motifs used are similar to those in other works made at Buda. One of its miniatures contains a representation of the peasant of the time (Fig. 33). Though in some of its minor ornamental elements the illumination of the Filipecz Pontifical displays a resemblance to the style of Francesco di Kastello, on the whole it suggests the work of another artist, as does also the magnificent title-page of the Trapezuntius Corvina Manuscript (Budapest, OSZK Clmae 281; Plate XXXIII).

The small Psalter containing two splendid border decorations, prepared for Urbanus Dóczi de Nagylucse, also belongs to this artistic circle (Budapest, OSZK Clmae 369; Plate XXXIV). The style leads directly to the outstanding achievement of the Buda workshop

Fidelium deus omnium conditor et redemptor
animabus famulorum famularumque tuarum:
remissionem cunctorum tribue peccatorum: ut indulgen
ciam quam semper optaverunt piis supplicacionibus
consequantur. Qui vivis. In adventu hymnus.

Conditor alme syderum eter

na lux credencium Christe redemptor

redemptor omnium exaudi preces supplicum. Qui con
dolens interitu mortis perire seculum salvasti mundum
languidum donans reis remedium. Vergente
mundi vespere uti sponsus de thalamo egressus
honestissima virginis matris clausula. Cuius
forti potencie genu curvantur omnia celestia terre
stria fatentur nutu subdita. Occasum sol custo
diens luna pallorem retinens candor in astris
relucens certos observat limites. Te deprecamur
hagye venture iudex seculi conserva nos in tempore
hostis a telo perfidi. Laus honor virtus gloria deo

of miniaturists, to the illumination of the Cassianus Manuscript. Unlike the vivid, bright, gaily-coloured decorations of Matthias's first heraldic painter and of Francesco di Kastello, this style of Buda is marked by the use of darker, duller colours. In the border-frame decorations a background of dark and deep red, blue, or green is relieved by painted gold vases, coloured balls, pearls, precious stones and scenes of children at play. In the five-volume Aristotle incunabulum, as also in some border-frame decorations of the Cassianus Manuscript, dark purple and black ground colours were to dominate, ornamented with extremely delicate floral motifs painted in gold. The illumination of the Cassianus Manuscript was finished after the death of Matthias for the Hungarian King Wladislas II; it contains the monogram of the eminent humanist, Felix Petancius Ragusinus, Matthias Corvinus's miniaturist.

In his work entitled *Hungaria*, Nicolaus Oláh, Archbishop of Esztergom, who had served King Wladislas as a page and had spent the years from 1510 to 1516 at the court, mentions Felix Petancius Ragusinus as a personal acquaintance, alluding to him as the "prefect" of King Matthias's court workshop of miniaturists. As stated in his account, Felix Petancius Ragusinus not only knew Greek, Latin, Chaldean and Arabic, but was also an authority on painting; moreover, as head of the workshop of Buda it was he who had to ensure that texts were copied accurately. Humanist, scholar, writer, diplomat, illuminator and miniaturist, Felix Petancius Ragusinus typified the many-sidedness of a man of the Renaissance. The extraordinary depth and range of his erudition is shown in a work which he wrote in the reign of Wladislas II, when the danger of a Turkish invasion was becoming increasingly acute. In order to avert the threat he proposed to launch an attack against the Turks and in 1502 he submitted to Wladislas II a plan of campaign *(Dissertatio de Itineribus Aggregiendi Turcam ad Vladislaum Hungariae et Bohemiae Regem)*. The text of this memorandum was printed and published by the German humanist Joannes Cuspinianus in 1522.

One of the most remarkable works of Felix Petancius Ragusinus was the *Genealogia Turcorum imperatorum* (Budapest, OSZK Clmae 378), which was also dedicated by its author to King Wladislas II. It is interesting that this manuscript was written not as a book but as a long scroll—a *rotulus* of antique form (2,170×395 mm)—which is decorated with portraits of Turkish sultans and viziers. In that age, apart from letters patent, scrolls were used only for the writing of Hebrew manuscripts. By his choice of this unusual form, Felix

36

Petancius Ragusinus evidently wished to emphasize the oriental character of his theme (Plate XLV). It is furthermore noteworthy that the text does not only give the genealogy of the emperors but also relates the history of the Turks. The decorations were done in the miniature workshop of Wladislas II, and the author's name, Felix Petancius Ragusinus, figures on the manuscript written in his own hand. There can be no doubt that Felix Petancius Ragusinus, a skilled and versatile painter, illuminated his work himself. On the scroll the portraits of Turkish sultans and viziers are presented in eight large and thirty-five small medallions which, in compliance with the demands of the scroll form, are painted in more dilute colours than the thick, opaque paint, more liable to peel off, which was usually employed for miniature painting at Buda. The representation of the sultans closes with the portrait of Bayazid II in a large medallion.

The miniatures picturing Turkish sultans in the *Genealogia Turcorum imperatorum* of Budapest bear a close relationship to the ornate miniatures in King Wladislas II's other manuscript on the theme of Turkey, the *Historia Turcica*, which is to be found in the Municipal

Library of Nuremberg. The portraits of Turkish sultans in its miniatures fully resemble those in the *Genealogia*. Felix Petancius Ragusinus may therefore be supposed to have been not only the author of the text of the Nuremberg *Historia Turcica*, but also the painter of its miniatures. The illumination of the *Genealogia* of Budapest shows remarkable qualities of design; there are two magnificent, exceedingly decorative flower motifs in the style of the miniature workshop in the period of Wladislas II.

Similar flowers are found in a liturgical work prepared at the close of the 15th century and in the opening years of the 16th—a Psalter containing the anthem of the Hungarian King St Ladislas (Esztergom, FK; Fig. 35). These motifs appear as typical ornamental elements in the border decoration of the Esztergom Missal, printed at Venice in 1498 at the expense of Johannes Paep, a bookseller of Buda; in this decoration the arms of Petrus Váradi, Archbishop of Kalocsa (1480–1501), are held by two kneeling angels (Budapest, OSZK Inc. 181).

Another remarkable and important work produced in Wladislas II's miniature workshop of Buda in the 1490s is folio 44 and folio 45 from a large and magnificent Antiphonary, of which the rest has been lost (Budapest, Museum of Fine Arts). On one of the folios (44v) the border-frame decoration is quite original and individual with an astonishing figured composition. In the ornate initial *S* on this page King David is seen praying, the representation of the male figure being characteristic of the workshop of Buda. The narrow upper edge of the border decoration is adorned with a pattern of golden palmettes against a blue background, executed in the style favoured by the Buda workshop. In the illumination framing the outer and lower edges of the page there are representations of the hermits St Anthony and St Paul. The border decoration also encloses a landscape, where shown are scenes of St Anthony's wanderings in

37

the desert and of his temptations. For the difficulties of composition presented by his theme the artist found an ingenious solution; his treatment, though slightly naive, has a broad epic quality. The composition is all the more fascinating as St Anthony is being tempted in the desert not by devils and monsters, but by mythical beings resembling centaurs (Plate XXXVII). They are clearly inspired by Dante's *Divine Comedy* and the host of centaurs appearing in the *Inferno*.

Already during the lifetime of Matthias Corvinus the style of the illuminators' workshop of Buda influenced the execution of some minor, less representative works. When we were speaking of Stephanus Nagylaki's small Breviary, produced in 1489, we pointed out that the decorations of this unassuming manuscript followed Gothic traditions, but that the miniaturist was also influenced by the Renaissance style of decoration which was favoured in the King's workshop. This influence increased in the reign of Wladislas II, and the small Prayer Book of Benigna Magyar, the wife of Pál Kinizsi, the great general who defeated the Turks, which used to belong to the Duke of Festetics of Keszthely (Budapest, OSZK MNY 73) was produced not later than 1494, and was decorated in mature Renaissance style.

It is astonishing that apart from sovereigns and prelates Benigna Magyar should have been the only secular person in Hungary whose splendidly illuminated manuscripts have come down to posterity. Her Prayer Book is adorned with beautiful border decorations, but this is not its only value. Unlike other illuminated manuscripts prepared in Hungary, its text was written not in Latin but in Hungarian, it is thus a precious relic of the old Hungarian language. Being written in Hungarian, it shows that Hungarian women said their prayers in their mother tongue, although for men a Latin education was obligatory in that age. The ornate title-page of the Prayer Book and several border decorations are executed in a style conforming to the trends followed by the workshop of Buda (Plate XXXVI). The style

38

of the border decorations, however, which are composed of flower motifs, is related not only to the miniature art of King Matthias's period, but also to the less carefully elaborated Renaissance decorations of the incunabulum of Esztergom, which was a missal illuminated in the years 1499 to 1501 for Petrus Váradi at the workshop of the Buda bookseller named Johannes Paep. Besides executing with evident pleasure compositions of figures, the artist who illuminated the Prayer Book of Benigna Magyar also sought to capture the natural beauty of landscape. The Holy Virgin painted with remarkable artistic skill in the miniature on the title-page, and the two kneeling angels with great wings who are holding the arms indicate that the master was influenced by the well-known sculptural works of the Renaissance court which was highly developed in the time of Matthias. Another small Hungarian Prayer Book of Benigna Magyar has also survived (Budapest, Library of the Hungarian Academy of Sciences M. Cod. 12° 2). This volume was made in 1513, but both the manuscript and some of its border decorations have come down to us in a mutilated condition.

In the opening decades of the 16th century, the provincial centres of Hungarian cultural life display, both in the temporal and the spiritual spheres, other influences than those of the Renaissance style prevalent in the royal miniature workshop of Buda. These varying styles were an inheritance from the Gothic; the new trends of style coming from Germany, Austria and Flanders are found curiously blended with Italian and Buda decorative motifs of a Renaissance character, as in the pages of an Evangelistary (Budapest, EK Cod. lat. 113) produced in the years from 1511 to 1515 at the Benedictine Abbey of Pannonhalma. This volume is a colligation consisting of two parts, the second being a Benedictionary prepared by Paulus Forgách of Losonc in 1515–16 at the Benedictine Abbey of Pannonhalma. From local allusions in the text, the first part of the manuscript may be supposed to have been written and illuminated at Pannonhalma. In the Evangelistary twenty-four pages are illuminated with border decoration and miniatures fitted into the initials, representing scenes from the life of Christ and pictures of several saints. The miniatures treat such themes as the Nativity (Plate XXXVIII), the Entry to Jerusalem, the Last Supper, the Resurrection, the Ascension, and the Pentecost; in the composition of these scenes the miniaturist took for his model the woodcuts of Dürer who treated similar themes in his series known as The Little Passion, from the years 1509 to 1511. The artist was also impressed by other works from

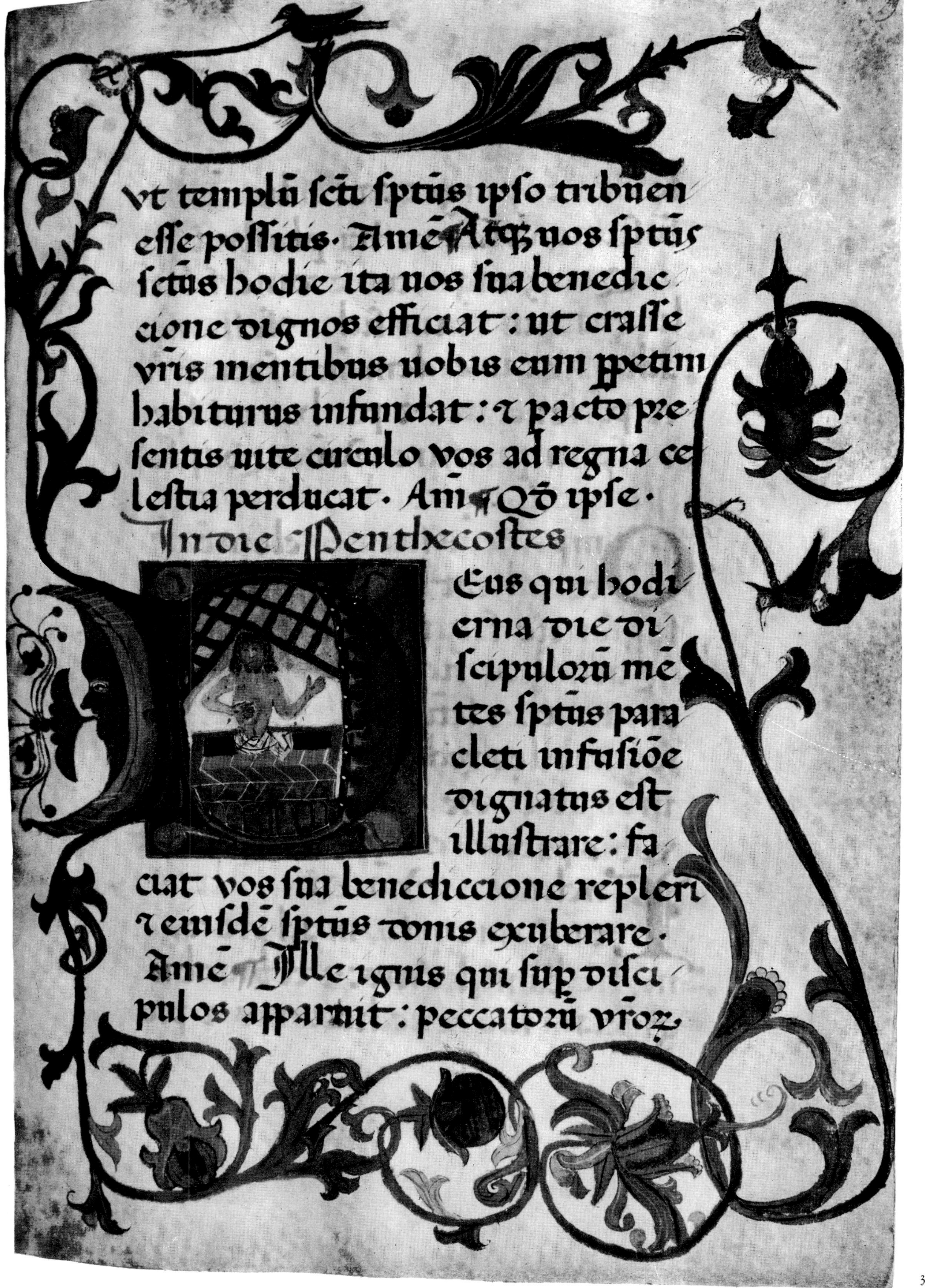

vt templū scti sp̄tus ipso tribuen
esse possitis. Amē. Atq3 uos sp̄tus
sctus hodie ita uos sua benedic
cione dignos efficiat: ut crasse
vris mentibus uobis eum ppetim
habiturus infundat: ⁊ pacto pre
sentis uite circulo vos ad regna ce
lestia perducat. Amē. Qd ipse.

In die Penthecostes

Deus qui hodi
erna die di
scipulorū mē
tes sp̄tus para
cleti infusiōe
dignatus est
illustrare: fa
ciat vos sua benediccione repleri
⁊ eiusdē sp̄tus donis exuberare.
Amē. Ille ignis qui sup disci
pulos apparuit: peccatorū vroꝝ

the circle of the young Dürer, namely the engravings in the Prayer Book of Basel, and also by an engraving of Schongauer; he assimilated these influences, and his style in the miniatures is harmonious and accomplished.

He displays less self-assurance in the painting of the ornate border decorations. Here he employs various foreign motifs, his choice clearly depending on the designs in the foreign manuscripts, since lost, which were available to him at that time in the monastery of Pannonhalma. Thus he uses the slender stylized leaves ending in lively spirals which were beloved by the Lower Austrian school of miniaturists, but combined them in a calmer and purer composition, enriched by tiny flowers and playful little *putti*. Elsewhere he paints in realistic style a varied profusion of gorgeous flowers, as if he preferred Flemish miniature art. Further, the influence of the Renaissance art of North Italy and Milan, as well as Buda, is indicated in the use of symmetrically arranged gold ornaments, pearls, garlands of leaves, and decorative foliated scrolls interspersed with little *putti* playing the flute.

The miniaturist does not hesitate to combine motifs of various ornamental styles; he places realistic roses among the interlaced lines and pointed leaves of Gothic scrolls, and little Italian *putti* among life-like Flemish flowers. The motif of the *putto* playing with a bear exhibits a relationship to the art of S. Stetner, an eminent master of Tyrolese miniature painting (Figs 37 and 38). The miniaturist of the Pannonhalma Evangelistary was, we see, an eclectic artist. Receptive to the various schools of European art and borrowing ornamental elements freely from different sources, he developed his own individual style. The illumination of the second part of the volume, the Forgách Benedictionary, on the other hand, is primitive, naive work, almost verging on folk art. The miniaturist evidently tried his best but he seems to have possessed little skill or ingenuity (Fig. 39); he clearly sought help in other men's work, and in one instance he took as his model a decoration of the Evangelistary, making a faithful but primitive copy.

Kindred in manner and conception is the illumination of another famous relic of the old Hungarian language, the so-called Jordánszky Manuscript (Esztergom, FK Ms. II. 1). Here the miniaturist endeavoured to make up for his lack of skill by ornate execution and even the use of gold. The manuscript, made in the years from 1516 to 1519, contains a Hungarian version of the Bible. The miniaturist's style is not unified: in the border decorations he made use of a variety of

um ce li et coram omnibus
viventibus cõfitebimur e i
quia fe cit nobis cum mise
ricordi am su am
De corpo re Christi
i ba uit e os
ex adi pe
frumenti al

motifs, following old models, particularly the works produced by the miniature workshop of Matthias Corvinus at Buda. The Renaissance motifs of the horn of plenty, vases and garlands are painted in vivid shades of red, yellow, blue and green; and the simple gaiety of these colours lends to the decorations a quality not far removed from folk art. The miniaturist's individual sense of design is most strikingly shown on the first page of the manuscript, where we find variegated ornamental motifs with braided and chequered patterns; in miniature painting these are unusual, even bizarre, and they were most probably borrowed from folk weaving. Nevertheless, the illumination of this manuscript was painted by a much more accomplished master than the miniaturist of the Forgách Manuscript, of which we have just spoken.

In this period a miniaturist was also active, between 1514 and 1524, in Transylvania at the court of Franciscus Várday, Bishop of Transylvania, who was a patron of the arts and a lover of books. This master decorated with coats of arms and miniatures the Várday Pontifical (Vienna, National Library Cod. 1799). Clearly, this cannot have been his only work and it may be assumed that he illuminated for Bishop Várday other manuscripts which have perished. Franciscus Várday is known to have taken part personally in putting down the peasant revolt headed by György Dózsa; and it was his vicar, Canon Stephanus Taurinus, who wrote a book on Dózsa's revolt entitled *Stauromachia*. It was printed in Vienna in 1519, and on its title-page is the earliest portrait of Dózsa; he is shown on a red-hot throne.

One of the finest fruits of Hungarian provincial miniature art is a large Gradual in two volumes, dating from 1518, which was made at Kassa for the St Elizabeth Parish Church, subsequently the cathedral of that town (Budapest, OSZK, Vol. I: Clmae 452; Vol. II: Clmae 172). The richly decorated volumes were later mutilated. The first volume now contains altogether three miniatures fitted into initials, and seven painted ornamental initials with border decoration, as well as innumerable calligraphic initials. In the second volume there are four miniatures inside initials, with border decoration, and fifteen painted initials. The date of illumination is to be found on folio 273 of the second volume. The date 1518 can be read in faded figures in the outer border decoration of the page (Fig. 43).

In the badly damaged miniatures of the Kassa Gradual are to be seen conventional representations of single figures of saints and also most expressive compositions of a very high quality on such themes

ri tu o glo riam et mag
num decorem impones su
In die
sancto
per e um Dominus
E ven tre
matris me
e vocavit me Do
minus no mine me o

as the Ascension (Vol. I, fol. 223), the Falling of the Manna (Vol. I, fol. 238v), and the Baptism of Christ (Vol. II, fol. 169v). All of them are gems of old Hungarian art.

In painting the Baptism of Christ the miniaturist threw off the constraint of traditions and did not employ the customary iconographic scheme. He simplified the composition that he might devote himself more freely to painting the background, the lovely landscape of the mountains surrounding the town of Kassa. The significance of the biblical scene, which is painted with great delicacy, is enhanced by the landscape and the black outlines of the towering trees. These are not the decoratively slender and softly swaying trees seen in ornamental motifs, but real trees, massive and living; and in painting the green bushes on the gently sloping hillside the artist strove to render living nature, the swift, rippling brook. The beautiful, balanced figures of Christ and John the Baptist are painted with that mellow
42 expressiveness characteristic of the 16th-century painting of Kassa with which the master's art, both in conception and style, is in complete harmony (Plate XL; Fig. 41).

Artistic sincerity of the highest quality characterizes the representation of the Falling of the Manna. The theme of the Jews collecting manna in the wilderness is also portrayed in a 15th-century triptych in Kassa Cathedral. The master of the Gradual did not follow the accepted iconography of this theme, but allowed his imagination full scope. He set the scene of the Falling of the Manna not in the desert, but in the hills outside Kassa. Nor did he paint a biblical picture of the Israelites watching in rapt attention a heavenly miracle, but a secular scene, nothing less than a genre painting of his own time. Though God the Father may be seen in the sky, the picture is not of the miraculous rain of manna, but of the workaday world of men.

Amidst the rich, green foliage of trees and bushes, on a yellow path bordered by green grass a Jew with a hat on his head and a fair-haired lad are crouching and stooping, gathering manna as if they were picking mushrooms. The main stress in the picture is on the figure of the long-bearded monk in the foreground who is collecting the manna in his habit. This figure recalls the hermits of the Cassianus Manuscript in Paris. In sharp contrast to this dignified figure, we see from the rear a man sitting on the grass and holding up a dish to catch the manna falling from the sky. In the valley in the background there is a view of the town of Kassa, painted in hazy, bluish, opalescent hues.

The striving of the artist in this miniature was in the first place to represent types characteristic of his environment, perhaps even portraits, and to show these figures in varied movement; and also he wished to perpetuate the landscape of Kassa. He has fully succeeded, and the realism of style and conception is hardly to be paralleled in Hungarian miniature art (Plate XXXIX; Fig. 40). The movement of the human figures and the richness of the landscape are brilliantly and truthfully rendered by the master of the Kassa Gradual.

To the work of border decoration he did not bring the same loving eagerness, although in the execution of floral ornamentation he displayed admirable variety. Gothic foliated elements, rippling, winding scrolls with stylized pointed leaves and flowers, bare branches and twigs still occur, but there is no longer the nervous restlessness of form typical of the 15th century. In the Gradual these Gothic elements are employed with a Renaissance sense of form, rising up from vases, to run along the margins. We also find the decorative elements of Renaissance miniature painting: sprays of palmette leaves calmly intersecting, garlands, golden fruit, vases, beaded tassels and ruffled ribbons. It would be going too far to look for foreign influences behind the Gothic decorative elements, since these had long been used in Hungarian Gothic art, as has been shown above (Fig. 42).

In the border decorations of the Kassa Gradual memories of Hungarian Gothic art are still alive, but they are mingled with Renaissance elements; and, what is more, they are already relegated to the background. Less finished in the presentation, the motifs of Renaissance ornamentation follow the style of the miniature workshop of Buda; but we also meet plainer and more commonplace Renaissance motifs such as were used in the workshop of a Buda bookseller in the opening years of the 16th century. Other decorative elements are also encountered—for instance, floral ornamentation inspired by the realism of Flemish art, which is unusual in the products of the Buda workshop. Roses with thorns on their stalks were painted also at Buda, but no scarlet cherries in pairs, no red rose-hips, green bean pods, yellow and blue pansies fully opened, grey serpents or dry branches. Instead of floral decoration, the miniaturist in one place painted a marsh marigold flowering in a peasant jug with a handle, and even the shadow cast by the jug can be seen on the white parchment. Such a style of representation virtually belongs to the domain of panel painting. Indeed, when he employs sketchy floral ornamentation the master is faithful to tradition, but his work lacks interest or vitality. He seems to have found it much more attractive and absorb-

43

ing to paint to the life flowers and fruits or a snake than to adorn the parchment with decorative foliated scrolls or Renaissance motifs of garlands of foliage and vases.

The miniaturist's fresh conception of nature and his striving for lifelike representation are arresting. In his painting both of fruits or flowers and of landscapes he manifested the same power of observation and profound sense of realism. In both volumes of the manuscript the same qualities are shown in the numerous calligraphic initials, including miniatures with such figured motifs as a man leading a lion, a prophet holding a roll of parchment, and the high priest Caiaphas, or with representations of animals: a duck, a horse, or a running hare, etc. The miniaturist of the Kassa Gradual never borrowed from the engravings in general circulation at the time; he always painted original compositions of great artistic skill and excellence.

From the close of the 15th century and in the course of the 16th, the copying of manuscripts was gradually superseded by the rapid advance of printing, and the engravings illustrating the increasing numbers of printed books exerted a strong influence on miniature art, panel painting, and also on wood carving. Miniaturists gladly made their work easier by borrowing the composition of engravings and imitating their biblical scenes. In the 16th century, miniaturists, even the most eminent masters, copied engravings. A Bohemian (Prague) miniaturist of Wladislas II followed, among others, the woodcuts of Wolgemut, while the master of the Pannonhalma Evangelistary drew upon the woodcuts of Dürer. At a much earlier date, in 1495, an excellent miniaturist of Georgius, Abbot of Topuszkó and Bishop of Rozsnyó (now Topusko, Yugoslavia, and Rožňava, Czechoslovakia) (1488–1498), who painted an elaborately illuminated Missal now in the Archiepiscopal Library of Zagreb (MR 354), borrowed and copied all the engravings of the German artist Master E. S. and Israhel van Meckenem.

Not a trace of such copying of woodcuts or engravings can be found in the art of the miniaturist who illuminated the Kassa Gradual. In this respect he resembles his contemporary, the outstanding artistic personality of the miniature workshop maintained at Buda by the court chancellery, the master of the Erdődy-Bakócz Manuscripts, who also avoided the imitation of woodcuts and engravings, although it was he who completed the unfinished illumination of the above-mentioned Missal of Georgius for Simon Erdődy-Bakócz, Bishop of Zagreb (1519–1543).

When we compare these two masters, we find that the artist of the Kassa Gradual gave expression in his miniatures to the peculiar character of Kassa painting which, advancing from the Late Gothic stage, developed a mature Renaissance style. The artist of the Erdődy-Bakócz Manuscripts, on the other hand, continued to use the ornamental methods and technique of Matthias Corvinus's miniature workshop of Buda; painting with a delicate technique and meticulous care, he shows a strong liking for lavish decoration and an evident desire to adorn his parchment with sumptuous border-frame decorations elaborated to the last detail.

44a

The master of the Erdődy-Bakócz Manuscripts was the last true artist of the style cultivated by the miniature workshop of the court of Buda; he represents at its peak the style which had flourished for half a century. He enriched Hungarian miniature art with new colours, new conceptions, new qualities. He was not only a miniaturist but also the heraldic painter of Wladislas II and Louis II; in this capacity he painted several fine letters patent between 1515 and 1525. As in the reign of Matthias, so also in the period of Wladislas II and Louis II a close cooperation may be noted between the chancellery's workshop of heraldic painters and the court workshop of miniaturists. The artist of the Erdődy-Bakócz Manuscripts must have been trained at these workshops, where exceedingly beautiful letters patent were painted in the time of Wladislas II. We may mention only the extremely delicate and lovely figure of the angel (Fig. 36) in the letters patent of the town of Kassa from 1502 (Košice, Town Archives), which recalls products of the Buda workshop—for instance, the angels holding the arms in the Cassianus Corvina Manuscript, and the decorative portrayal of the women of the harem in the *Historia Turcica* of Nuremberg.

44b

44c

In the representation of lightly-dressed female figures and in some motifs of ornamentation the master of the Erdődy-Bakócz Manuscripts followed the style of Felix Petancius Ragusinus who had carried on these traditions of Buda. He painted several letters patent at the workshop of heraldic painters, including those of Dorottya Kanizsay (1519), the family Kállay Vitéz (1521), the family Ghymesi Forgách, and others. Two manuscripts of his with unfinished illumination are known: both bear the mitred coat of arms of the Erdődy-Bakócz family, indicating the owner. Thomas Bakócz, Archbishop of Esztergom (1498–1521), who had played a leading role in Hungarian public life during the reign of King Matthias, became Archbishop under Wladislas II, and Cardinal in 1500; since he did not thereafter

45

use his episcopal arms, these two manuscripts were doubtlessly prepared for his nephew, Simon Erdődy, Bishop of Zagreb. The manuscripts were actually made during the episcopate of Simon Erdődy-Bakócz at Zagreb, and illuminated in the style of the letters patent painted at Buda between 1519 and 1525; hence they must have been the property of Simon Erdődy. In the literature on the subject it has several times been suggested that these manuscripts may date from the time when Archbishop Bakócz was Bishop of Eger. Curiously enough, although Archbishop Bakócz had many residences built and possessed unusual artistic sense, not one richly illuminated manuscript is known to have belonged to him except the Ransanus Corvina Manuscript (Budapest, OSZK Clmae 249) which was prepared for King Matthias in Italy and later presented to Bakócz. There can be no doubt that Bakócz employed miniaturists, but the manuscripts illuminated to his order have been destroyed or their present whereabouts are unknown.

The second volume of the large unfinished Gradual in two volumes (Esztergom, FK) prepared for Simon Erdődy, that is to say for Zagreb Cathedral, is undecorated, with blank spaces instead of initials. The illumination of the first volume is also incomplete, only the title-page having been finished; there are also three unfinished border decorations, while miniatures are to be found only in two finished initials, in one of which there is only a design. The miniaturist also painted several plain, smaller initials, decorated with floral motifs. Later, in 1557, when the archiepiscopal see was transferred from Esztergom to Nagyszombat (now Trnava, Czechoslovakia) in order to place it outside the reach of the advancing Turkish forces, a miniaturist of Nicolaus Oláh, Archbishop of Esztergom, Master I. K., made several drawings of decorations, but he also did not complete the illumination of the volume (Figs. 44a–c, 45).

The title-page of the Esztergom Gradual is most richly decorated (Plate XLI); as in the Philostratus Corvina Manuscript, the text and the musical notes are written in gold, while the notation lines are drawn in red on a blue ground. The page is enclosed in a rich border decoration, with representations of God the Father and the Annunciation in three medallions. In the decoration of the lower edge the piscopal arms of Bakócz are held by two charming angels with large wings. The initial *A* contains a representation of King David at prayer (Plate XLI). An unfinished border-frame decoration, similar to that of the title-page, may be found in the manuscript on folio 11v, where the arms are held by the two cardinal virtues, Fortitude and

Prudence (?) (Plate XLII). In the medallions of this incomplete border-frame decoration there are representations of the evangelists Mark, Luke and John, of Pope Gregory, of St Jerome, and of the Annunciation to the Shepherds, which bears witness to close observation of nature and to the use of motifs from the life of the people. In hilly, rolling country a shepherd in the foreground is lying on the grass, resting on his elbow with his pipe in his hand, while a white dog sprawls at his feet. In the background another shepherd is standing among his grazing flock, leaning on his crook; both men are gazing at the angel appearing in the sky.

46a

The other work of the miniaturist who illuminated the Erdődy-Bakócz Manuscripts, which is found in the Archiepiscopal Library of Zagreb (MR 354), is also most interesting. In his work on the unfinished Missal made for Georgius, Abbot of Topuszkó and Bishop of Rozsnyó, he continued the style of the illumination executed for Simon Erdődy-Bakócz. But he did not finish the decoration of this volume either—he may have died before he could accomplish the task. The Zagreb Missal nevertheless contains a much larger number of border decorations than does the Esztergom Missal, and also a valuable Canon covering a whole page which movingly represents the Crucifixion; there are also several miniatures on biblical themes. Here a continuity of the Renaissance miniature art cultivated in the reign of King Matthias is still clearly discernible in the master's style, particularly in the ornamental design of ribbons which runs between the columns of the text, and in the slightly Gothic, small pointed leaves wound around it, a motif alien to Italian Renaissance miniature painting.

The miniaturist of the Erdődy-Bakócz Manuscripts seems to have cherished a liking for figures as ornamental elements, of which he has made remarkable use in his border decorations. Among a rich fabric of decorative flowers and foliated design he has inserted tiny *putti* with ruddy cheeks and rainbow wings, delightful female figures in light raiment, angels, and Tritons with fishes' tails, and in some of the initials he has painted dragons or dolphins. There are realistic pink roses among the flowers. His characteristic figures have their heads turned to one side with gentle grace. Gold is richly applied in these decorations. The initials, executed in prismatic patterns on a pure gold background, are adorned with blue, pink and green leaves set off by deep golden shading. In general, the artist's works are dominated by these three colours, in addition to the typical carmine, purple and scarlet tints. These colours lend a deep, warm tone to the

46b

illumination. The grounds of initials and border decorations are enlivened by graceful arabesques painted in gold, by vertical dotted lines or a thin black netting.

Since the miniaturist of the Erdődy-Bakócz Manuscripts did not complete his work on the Esztergom Gradual nor on the Zagreb Missal, the places of the medallions remained blank and unadorned in many border decorations. In the Zagreb Missal these spaces were later filled by an excellent master with magnificent, realistic representations of landscapes. Zagreb scholars regard the monogram to be found in the manuscript as evidence that these landscapes are the work of the eminent Croatian artist Giulio Clovio, painted when he was a young man. He was then in the service of Simon Erdődy and there is evidence of his having visited Buda in 1524. Like Simon Erdődy, Giulio Clovio, too, fought in the disastrous battle of Mohács in 1526. In any event, this artist did not finish the illumination of the Zagreb Manuscript, and in its pages the still later work of a fourth miniaturist may be distinguished.

Finally, mention must be made of one more elaborately illuminated work produced by the court workshop of Buda, a volume prepared for Franciscus Perényi, Bishop of Várad (1514–1526), the son of the palatine Emericus Perényi and his wife, the famous Dorottya Kanizsay. Young Franciscus Perényi fell in the battle of Mohács. The book decorated for him at the miniaturists' workshop of Buda was not a manuscript but an incunabulum (Győr, Episcopal Library): the Esztergom Missal printed at Venice in 1498 to the order of Johannes Paep, a bookseller of Buda. Numerous parchment folios of this Missal were given frames of dainty decorations while its woodcuts were coloured, the technique employed being one practised by the Renaissance miniaturists of Buda.

The border decorations of the Perényi Missal incunabulum belong to the mature products of the miniature workshop of Buda. They were painted at a time when ornamental Renaissance motifs were mingled with realistic representations of flowers and foliage (Plate XLIII). The illumination of this Missal possesses special value because the volume contains a representation of the Dance of Death; so far as we know, this is the first, and some believe it to be the only, occurrence of this theme in Hungarian miniature art.

The figure of grinning Death had been introduced earlier into Hungarian miniature art; it is to be found twice in Dominicus Kálmáncsehi's Prayer Book, which dates from 1492 and is now preserved in Paris (folios 85v and 88). In the Perényi Missal, in the lower border decoration of folio 218, the miniaturist depicted between two death's-heads a scene in the true manner of Holbein, in which Death, holding a sand-glass, carries off a youthful-looking bishop (Plate XLIV). It was, perhaps, not only the representation of the Dance of Death in other countries which inspired the artist to portray this theme; he may have been drawn to it because of the desperate situation in his own country after Dózsa's revolt, and the increasing threat of a Turkish invasion. The Missal subsequently came into the possession of several prelates in succession, including Nicolaus Oláh, Archbishop of Esztergom, all of whom added to its decorations.

Hungarian miniature painting may be said to have now practically reached the end of its history. Having begun to decline with the introduction of printing, it now continued only in a rudimentary form. The Turkish occupation of Hungary naturally contributed to its final disappearance, but the principal cause was the extensive use of printing. Instead of manuscripts and incunabula, miniaturists decorated the letters patent of the court chancellery, and painted pontifical arms for archbishops and bishops. The celebrated and brilliant typographer Georgius Bocskay (he died in 1575), secretary of the chancellery of three Habsburg monarchs at Vienna in the second half of the 16th century, adorned letters patent; his elaborate ornaments were executed with superb technique. In 1562 he prepared for King Ferdinand a Writing Pattern Book (Vienna, National Library Cod. Ser. n. 2664), in which he not only showed the styles of lettering used in the old manuscripts and initials, one more handsome than the other, but he also painted artistic ornamentations, inspired by the foliated and interlaced or braided scrolls of various ages and styles, as well as minor figured motifs, female nudes, and also animals (Figs. 46a–c).

At Nagyszombat, as already mentioned, Nicolaus Oláh also employed miniaturists, and works executed by miniaturists after his death in 1568 have also come down to us from the second half of the 16th century. One of these works, known to have been made at Nagyszombat and noteworthy from an iconographic aspect on account of its novel conception, is the illumination on the parchment title-page of the Zagreb Missal. The Missal was printed in Venice in 1511, and the parchment title-page was illuminated in 1592 for Johannes Chereődi, Bishop of Pécs, governor of the archbishopric of Esztergom. On its upper border there stands on one side of the episcopal arms the figure of Bishop Adalbert, the saint after whom the

46c

ancient cathedral of Esztergom had been named; on the other side, we see once more after a long lapse of time, as the closing motif, one may say, of the history of Hungarian miniature painting, a representation of the founder of Hungary, King Stephen (Fig. 47).

The miniaturist painted St Adalbert in full pontificals, but the representation of King Stephen, though the theme is ecclesiastical, is far from that of a haloed saint. This was the time of ravages by the Turks and of the rule of the Habsburgs, and the artist was perhaps influenced also by Protestant religious movements; with clear national consciousness the miniaturist painted the first King of Hungary, St Stephen, as a mighty king, wearing a braided coat in the contemporary taste. Thus when its day was done, Hungarian miniature art returned, as it were, to the heroic ideals of the Anjou period, to the conception which had inspired the decorations of the Illuminated Chronicle.

47

BIBLIOGRAPHY

D'Ancona, Paolo–Aeschlimann, Erardo: *Dictionnaire des Miniaturistes.* Milan, 1949, second edition.

"Ausstellung Barcelona." *Pantheon.* 1929, p. 572.

Balogh, Jolán (Jolanda): "A madocsai apát, a királyi könyvek miniátora" [The Abbot of Madocsa, Miniaturist of the Royal Books]. *Henszlmann-Lapok,* 1927, No. 5. – *Adatok Milánó és Magyarország kulturális kapcsolatainak történetéhez – Contributi alla storia delle relazioni d'arte e di cultura tra Milano e l'Ungheria.* Budapest, 1928. – *Az erdélyi renaissance* [Renaissance Art in Transylvania]. Vol. I. Kolozsvár, 1943. – "Mátyás király ismeretlen miniatúra arcképe" [Unknown Miniature Portrait of King Matthias]. *Művészettörténeti Értesítő,* 1956, pp. 132–134. – "Ercole Roberti a Buda." *Acta Historiae Artium Academiae Scientiarum Hungaricae,* 1959, Nos. 3–4, pp. 277–281. – "A renaissance művészete Magyarországon" [Renaissance Art in Hungary]. In: *A magyarországi művészet története. I. A magyarországi művészet a honfoglalástól a XIX. századig* [History of Hungarian Art, Vol. I. Hungarian Art from the Magyar Conquest to the 19th Century]. Budapest, 1964, third (revised) edition.

Bartoniek, Emma: *Codices latini medii aevi.* Vol. I. *Codices manuscripti latini.* Budapest, 1940. (Hungarian National Museum, National Széchényi Library, Index XII.)

Barzon, A.: *Codici miniati. Biblioteca Capitolare della Cattedrale di Padova.* Padua, 1950, pp. 25–28.

Berkovits, Ilona (Elena, Helene): *A budapesti Egyetemi Könyvtár Dante-kódexe és a XIII. és XIV. századi velencei miniatúrafestészet története* [The Dante Manuscript of the University Library, Budapest, and the History of 13th and 14th-century Venetian Miniature Painting]. Budapest, 1928. Dissertation. – "A miniatűrfestészet" [Miniature Painting]. *Műgyűjtő,* 1928, pp. 176–177. – "A Budapesti Egyetemi Könyvtár Pannonhalmi kódexe" [The Pannonhalma Manuscript of the University Library, Budapest]. *Magyar Művészet,* 1929, pp. 181–196. – Review of the work of Hermann, Hermann Julius: *Die italienischen Handschriften des Dugento und Trecento, 2. Magyar Könyvszemle,* 1930, pp. 174–179. – "Un codice dantesco nella Biblioteca della R. Univ. di Budapest." *Pubblicazioni dell'Istituto Storia dell'arte e di Archeologia Cristiana presso la R. Università "Pietro Pázmány" di Budapest,* 1931. – "A budapesti Egyetemi Könyvtár festett kéziratainak egy csoportja" [A Group of the Illuminated Manuscripts of the University Library, Budapest]. *Magyar Könyvszemle,* 1931, pp. 1–22. – "A pécsi püspöki könyvtár festett kéziratai és ősnyomtatványai" [The Illuminated Manuscripts and Incunabula of the Episcopal Library of Pécs]. *Magyar Könyvszemle,* 1937, pp. 35–49. – "A Képes Krónika és Szent István királyt ábrázoló miniatúrái" [The Illuminated Chronicle and Its Miniatures Representing St Stephen]. *Magyar Könyvszemle,* 1938, pp. 1–20. – "Négyszázötven éves vándorlás után hazatér a Kálmáncsehi-kódex" [After Wandering for Four Hundred and Fifty Years, the Kálmáncsehi Manuscript Returns Home]. *Magyar Nemzet,* February 12, 1939. – "Felice Petanzio Ragusino, capo della bottega di miniatori di Mattia Corvino." *Archivio di Scienze, Lettere ed Arti della Società Italo-Ungherese Mattia Corvino.* Supplemento a *Corvina,* 1940, pp. 35–84. – "A Szépművészeti Múzeum Grafikai Osztályának LXXVII. kiállítása" [77th Exhibition of the Graphic Department of the Museum of Fine Arts]. *Magyar Könyvszemle,* 1941, pp. 293–296. – "La mostra della Miniatura a Budapest, Manuscritti e miniature nei secoli X–XX." *Corvina,* 1941, pp. 390–398. – "Az Esztergomi Ulászló Graduale" [The Esztergom Gradual of King Wladislas]. *Magyar Könyvszemle,* 1941, pp. 342–353. – "Miniatori Ungheresi nel '*Dictionnaire des Miniaturistes*'." *Corvina,* 1941, pp. 255–281. – "La pietra sepolcrale di un umanista ferrarese a Cassovia." *Archivio di Scienze, Lettere ed Arti della Società Italo-Ungherese Mattia Corvino.* Supplemento a *Corvina,* 1941, pp. 164–174. – *La miniatura nella corte di Mattia Corvino. Ferrara ed il rinascimento ungherese.* Budapest, 1941. (Biblioteca della "Mattia Corvino" No. 10.) – "A Kassai Graduale és a XVI. századi kassai festészet" [The Kassa Gradual and 16th-century Kassa Painting]. *Gerevich Tibor Emlékkönyv* [Studies in Honour of Tibor Gerevich]. Budapest, 1942, pp. 64–86. – "A magyar miniatúrafestészet kezdetei. Az Árpád-kor" [The Beginnings of Hungarian Miniature Painting. The Period of the House of Árpád]. *Magyarságtudomány,* 1942, pp. 485–519. – "Mátyás király 'állítólagos' miniátorai. Válasz Gulyás Pálnak" [The "Alleged" Miniaturists of King Matthias. A Reply to Pál Gulyás]. *Magyar Könyvszemle,* 1942, pp. 153–161. – "Várday Ferenc pontificáléja Bécsben" [Franciscus Várday's Pontifical in Vienna]. *Magyar Könyvszemle,* 1942, pp. 253–260. – "Kolostori kódexfestészetünk a XIV. században" [Hungarian Monastic Miniature Painting in the 14th Century]. *Magyar Könyvszemle,* 1943, pp. 347–362. – "Magyar vonatkozású XIV. századi kéziratok a bécsi Nemzeti Könyvtárban" [14th-century Manuscripts Relating to Hungary in the National Library of Vienna]. *Magyar Könyvszemle,* 1943, pp. 67–68. – "Egy Corvin-kódex származása – Mátyás király követe Franciaországban" [The Origin of a Corvina Manuscript – King Matthias's Emissary in France]. *Magyar Könyvszemle,* 1945, pp. 22–37. – *La miniatura ungherese nel periodo degli Angiovini,* Rome, 1947. (Biblioteca dell'Accademia d'Ungheria in Roma. Nuova Serie, 5.) – "Une Ambassade hongroise en France, 1487." *Revue d'histoire comparée,* 1948, pp. 242–253. – "A kódexfestészet emlékei a Főszékesegyházi Könyvtárban" [Illuminated Manuscripts in the Cathedral Library]. *Magyarország Műemléki Topográfiája, I. Esztergom Műemlékei* [Topography of Art Monuments in Hungary. I. Art Monuments of Esztergom]. Budapest, 1948, pp. 290–371. – The Headwords of Hungarian Miniaturists in

D'Ancona, Paolo–Aeschlimann, Erardo: *Dictionnaire des Miniaturistes*. Milan, 1949, second edition. – "A magyar feudális társadalom tükröződése a Képes Krónikában" [The Picture of Hungarian Feudal Society in the Illuminated Chronicle]. *Századok*, 1953, pp. 72–107. – "Mostra storica nazionale della miniatura". Review in *Magyar Könyvszemle*, 1956, pp. 91–93. – "A Képes Krónika művészettörténeti jelentősége" [The Significance of the Illuminated Chronicle in Art History]. *Képes Krónika. Kálti Márk Krónikája a magyarok tetteiről. – Chronicon Pictum Marci de Kalt. Chronica de Gestis Hungarorum*. Budapest, 1959, pp. 29–45, 239–248. – "Egy Korvina-miniatúra" [A Miniature of a Corvina Manuscript]. *Művészettörténeti Értesítő*, 1959, pp. 250–259. – "Una miniatura della Biblioteca Corvina." *Acta Historiae Artium Academiae Scientiarum Hungaricae*, 1960, pp. 79–90. – "Die kunsthistorische Bedeutung der Bilderchronik." *Die ungarische Bilderchronik – Chronica de Gestis Hungarorum*. Budapest, 1961, pp. 31–61, 307–317. – *A magyarországi Corvinák*. Budapest, 1962. – *Illuminated Manuscripts from the Library of Matthias Corvinus*. Budapest, 1964. – *Corvinen. Bilderhandschriften aus der Bibliothek des Königs Matthias Corvinus*. Berlin, 1963. – *Miniature del Rinascimento nella Biblioteca di Mattia Corvino*. Milan, 1964. – *Corviniana Iluminowane Rekopisy Biblioteki Króla Macieja Korwina*. Wrocław, 1964. – "Új Corvina Magyarországon" [A New Corvina Manuscript in Hungary]. *A könyv*, 1964, p. 259, and *Magyar Grafika*, 1964, pp. 265–266. – "A zágrábi miniatúrakiállítás" [Exhibition of Miniatures in Zagreb]. *Magyar Könyvszemle*, 1965, pp. 268–271. – "A budapesti Dante-kódex miniatúrái" [The Miniatures of the Budapest Dante Manuscript]. Dante: *Isteni színjáték* [The Divine Comedy]. Budapest, 1965. – *Il Codice Dantesco di Budapest. – Italia ed Ungheria. Dieci secoli di rapporti letterari*. Budapest, 1967, pp. 45–57.

Buberl, Paul: *Die illuminierten Handschriften in Steiermark*. Leipzig, 1911, pp. 17–33. (*Beschreibendes Verzeichnis der illuminierten Handschriften in Österreich*. Vol. IV.)

Csapodi, Csaba: "Mikor szűnt meg Mátyás király könyvfestő műhelye?" [When Did King Matthias's Miniature Workshop Cease to Be Active?] (*Publicationes Bibliothecae Academiae Scientiarum Hungaricae* No. 24.), Budapest, 1963.

Dercsényi, Dezső: *Nagy Lajos kora* [The Age of Louis the Great]. Budapest, 1941. – "Manuscrit hongrois du Moyen Age en Amérique." *Nouvelle Revue de Hongrie*, 1942, pp. 109–117. – "Nekcsei Dömötör Bibliája a washingtoni Library of Congressben" [The Bible of Demetrius Nekcsei in the Washington Library of Congress]. *Magyar Könyvszemle*, 1942, pp. 113–125. – "A román kor művészete Magyarországon" [Romanesque Art in Hungary]. In: *A magyarországi művészet története. I. A magyarországi művészet a honfoglalástól a XIX. századig* [History of Hungarian Art, Vol. I. Hungarian Art from the Magyar Conquest to the 19th Century]. Budapest, 1964, third (revised) edition. – "The Illuminated Chronicle and Its Age." In: *The Illuminated Chronicle*, Budapest, 1969, pp. 13–57.

Falvi, Zoltán–Mezey, László: *Codex Albensis. Ein Antiphonar aus dem 12. Jahrhundert*. Budapest, 1963. (Monumenta Hungariae Musica, Vol. I.)

Fraknói, Vilmos–Fógel, József–Gulyás, Pál–Hoffmann, Edith: *Bibliotheca Corvina, Mátyás király budai könyvtára* [Bibliotheca Corvina, the Buda Library of King Matthias]. Budapest, 1927. – In Italian: Fraknói, Guglielmo–Fógel, Giuseppe–Gulyás, Paolo–Hoffmann, Edit: *Bibliotheca Corvina, la Biblioteca di Mattia Corvino re d'Ungheria*. Budapest, 1927.

Fraknói, Guillaume–Gottlieb, Théodore: *Manuscrit enluminé d'un prélat hongrois à la Bibliothèque Beatty à Londres*. (No date and place of publication.)

Gantner, Joseph: *Konrad Witz*. Vienna, 1942. – *Kunstgeschichte der Schweiz*, Vol. II. *Die gotische Kunst*. Frauenfeld, 1947.

Genthon, István: "Magyar művészek Ausztriában a mohácsi vészig. A magyar festészet története" [Hungarian Artists in Austria until the Battle of Mohács. History of Hungarian Painting]. *Szépművészetek könyve* [Book of Fine Arts]. Budapest, 1940. – "Budai emlékek szerte a világban" [Relics of Buda in Various Parts of the World]. *Budapest*, 1946, No. 7.

Gerevich, Ilona: "Vásári Miklós két kódexe" [Two Manuscripts of Nicolaus Vásári]. *Művészettörténeti Értesítő*, 1957, pp. 133–137.

Gerevich, Tibor (Tiberio): "A miniatűrfestészet, tekintettel a Corvin kódexekre" [Miniature Painting with Special Reference to Corvina Manuscripts]. *A Magyar Nemzeti Múzeum 1911. évi jelentése* [The 1911 Report of the Hungarian National Museum], pp. 282–291. – *A régi magyar művészet európai helyzete* [The Position of Old Hungarian Art in Europe]. Budapest, 1924. – *L'arte antica ungherese*. Rome, 1929. – *Magyarország román kori emlékei* [Romanesque Art in Hungary]. Budapest, 1938, pp. 229–235. – "A gótika művészete Magyarországon" [Gothic Art in Hungary]. In: *A magyarországi művészet története. I. A magyarországi művészet a honfoglalástól a XIX. századig* [History of Hungarian Art, Vol. I. Hungarian Art from the Magyar Conquest to the 19th Century]. Budapest, 1964, third (revised) edition.

Gulyás, Pál: "Mátyás király állítólagos miniátorai" [The Alleged Miniaturists of King Matthias]. *Magyar Könyvszemle*, 1942, pp. 11–17.

Güntherová, Alžběta–Mišianik, Ján: *Stredoveká knižná mal'ba Slovensku*. Bratislava, 1961. – *Illuminierte Handschriften aus der Slowakei*. Prague, 1962.

Harrsen, Meta: *The Nekcsei–Lipócz Bible. Fourteenth Century Manuscript from Hungary in the Library of Congress*. Washington, 1949. – *Central European Manuscripts in the Pierpont Morgan Library*. New York, 1958.

Hermann, Hermann Julius: "Die frühmittelalterlichen Handschriften des Abendlandes." *Beschreibendes Verzeichnis der illuminierten Handschriften in Österreich*. N. S. Vol. I, Part 1. – "Die deutschen romanischen Handschriften." *Beschreibendes Verzeichnis der illuminierten Handschriften in Österreich*. N. S. Vol. I, Part 2. – Die italienischen Handschriften des Dugento und Trecento. 2. Oberitalienische Handschriften der zweiten Hälfte des XIV. Jahrhunderts." *Beschreibendes Verzeichnis der illuminierten Handschriften in Österreich*. N. S. Vol. V, Part 2. – "Die italienischen Handschriften des Dugento und Trecento. 3. *Beschreibendes Verzeichnis der illuminierten Handschriften in Österreich*. N. S. Vol. V, Part 3.

Hevesy, André de: "Le Bréviaire de Sigismund de Luxembourg." *Bulletin de la Société française de reproductions de manuscrits à peintures*. Paris, 1911. – *La bibliothèque du roi Matthias Corvin*. Paris, 1923.

Hoffmann, Edith: "Nagylucsei Orbán könyvtárának maradványai" [Remnants of the Library of Urbanus de Nagylucse]. *Magyar Bibliofil Szemle*, 1924, pp. 167–168. –

"Der künstlerische Schmuck der Corvin-Codices." *Belvedere*, 1925, pp. 130–135. – "Mátyás király budai műhelyének egyik címerfestője" [A Heraldic Painter of King Matthias's Buda Workshop]. *Magyar Könyvszemle*, 1925, pp. 170–175. – "Középkori könyvkultúránk néhány fontos emlékéről" [A Few Important Relics of Hungarian Medieval Literary Culture]. *Magyar Könyvszemle*, 1925, pp. 47–51. – "Henrik csukárdi plébános miniator" [The Miniaturist Henry, Parish Priest of Csukárd]. *A Szépművészeti Múzeum Évkönyve* [Year-book of the Budapest Museum of Fine Arts], 1924–1926, pp. 74–90. – *A Nemzeti Múzeum Széchényi Könyvtárának illuminált kéziratai* [Illuminated Manuscripts of the National Széchényi Library]. Budapest, 1928. (Publications of the National Széchényi Library Vol. I.) – *Régi magyar bibliofilek* [Old Hungarian Bibliophiles]. Budapest, 1929. – "A Bécsből hazakerült műkincsek kiállítása a Nemzeti Múzeumban, III: Kéziratok" [Exhibition of the Art Treasures Returned Home from Vienna at the National Museum. Part III: Manuscripts]. *Magyar Művészet*, 1933, pp. 292–296. – "Franciscus de Kastello Ithallico de Mediolano és szerepe a budai könyvfestő műhelyben" [Franciscus de Kastello Ithallico de Mediolano and His Role in the Miniaturists' Workshop of Buda]. *Magyar Művészet*, 1933, pp. 42–46. – "Die Bücher Ludwigs des Grossen und die ungarische Bilderchronik." *Zentralblatt für Bibliothekswesen*, 1936, pp. 633–666. – *Pozsony a középkorban. Elfelejtett művészek. Elpusztult emlékek* [Pozsony in the Middle Ages. Forgotten Artists. Destroyed Monuments of Art]. Budapest, 1939. – "Mátyás király könyvtára" [The Library of King Matthias]. *Mátyás király Emlékkönyv* [Studies in the Memory of King Matthias]. Budapest, 1940, Vol. II, pp. 251–277. – *Kéziratok és miniatúrák. Országos Magyar Szépművészeti Múzeum. A Grafikai Osztály LXXVII. kiállítása* [Manuscripts and Miniatures. Museum of Fine Arts. 77th Exhibition of the Graphic Art Department]. Budapest, 1941.

HOLTER, KURT: *Die Wiener Buchmalerei. Geschichte der bildenden Kunst in Wien.* Vol. II, *Gotik*. Vienna, no date.

HOLTER, KURT–OETTINGER, KARL: "Les Principaux manuscrits à peintures de la Bibliothèque Nationale de Vienne: Manuscrits allemands." *Bulletin de la Société française de reproductions de manuscrits à peintures.* XXI, 1938.

HORVÁTH, HENRIK: *Zsigmond király és kora* [King Sigismund and His Period]. Budapest, 1937.

KNIEWALD, DRAGUTIN (KÁROLY): "A 'Hahóti kódex' (zágrábi MR 126 kézirat) jelentősége a magyarországi liturgia szempontjából. Kühár Flóris kiegészítésével" [Significance of the "Hahót Manuscript" from the Point of View of Hungarian Liturgy. Completed by Flóris Kühár]. *Magyar Könyvszemle*, 1938, pp. 97–112. – "A zágrábi érseki könyvtár MR 126 (XI. sz.) jelzésű Sacramentáriumának magyar rétege a MR 67. sz. zágrábi Breviárium (XIII. sz.) megvilágításában. A magyarországi liturgia legrégibb emléke" [The Hungarian Stratum of the 11th-century Sacramentary Marked MR 126 in the Archiepiscopal Library, Zagreb, in the Light of the 13th-century Zagreb Breviary, Marked MR 67. The Oldest Relic of Hungarian Liturgy]. *Pannonhalmi Szemle*, 1938, pp. 36–54. – *Zagrebački liturgyski kodeksi XI–XV stoljica.* Zagreb, 1940. – "Misal Časmanskog prepošta Jurja de Topusco i zagrebačkog biskupa Šimuna Erdődy." *RAD* (Zagreb), 1940, pp. 45–84. – „Kálmáncsehi Domonkos zágrábi misekönyve" [The Zagreb Missal of Dominicus Kálmáncsehi]. *Magyar Könyvszemle*, 1943, pp. 1–15. – "Sitnoslikar dubrovčanin Feliks Petančič – Der Miniaturmaler Felix Ragusinus Petantius." Zagreb, 1958. *Tkalčičevog Zbornika*, Vol. II, pp. 55–90. – "Feliks Petančič 1502 o putewima kojima valja napasti Turke." *Vesnik Vojnog mureja v Beograd*, 1958, pp. 25–58. – *Feliks Petančič Njegova Djela.* Académie Serbe des Sciences et des Arts, Monographies, Tome CCCL, No. 12. Belgrade, pp. 1–102.

LEVÁRDY, FERENC: "Il Leggendario Ungherese degli Angio conservato nella Biblioteca Vaticana, nel Morgan Library e nell'Ermitage." *Acta Historiae Artium Academiae Scientiarum Hungaricae*, 1963, pp. 75–138.

MAYER, AUGUST: "Eine oesterreichische Miniaturenhandschrift in Granada." *Belvedere*, 1929, pp. 423–424.

MEZEY, LADISLAUS: *Codices latini medii aevi Bibliothecae Universitatis Budapestiensis.* Budapest, 1961.

MIHALIK, ALESSANDRO: "Gioielli di Santa Elisabetta d'Ungheria a Udine ed a Cividale." *Corvina*, 1935.

Minijatura u Jugoslaviji. Muzej za umjetnost i Obrt. Zagreb, 1964, April–June.

Mostra Storica Nazionale della Miniatura. Palazzo di Venezia. Roma. Catalogue. Florence, 1954, second edition.

OETTINGER, KARL: "Der Illuminator Michael." *Die Graphischen Künste*, LVI, 1933. – "Der Illuminator Nicolaus." *Jahrbuch der Preussischen Kunstsammlungen.* LIV, 1933.

PATAKY, DÉNES: *A magyar rajzművészet.* Budapest, 1960, pp. 6–8. – *Hungarian Drawings and Water-colours.* Budapest, 1961. – *Zeichnung und Aquarell in Ungarn. Budapest*, 1961. – *Vengerskie Risunki i Akvareli.* Budapest, 1961.

PÉTER, ANDRÁS: *A magyar művészet története* [History of Hungarian Art]. Vol. I. Budapest, 1930.

PORCHER, JEAN: *Manuscrits à peintures offerts à la Bibliothèque Nationale par le Comte Guy du Boisrouvray.* Paris, 1961.

RADÓ, POLYCARPUS: *Répertoire hymnologique des manuscrits liturgiques dans les bibliothèques publiques de Hongrie.* Budapest, 1945. (Publications of the National Széchényi Library, Vol. XX.) – *Libri liturgici manuscripti bibliothecarum Hungariae.* Budapest, 1947. (Publications of the National Széchényi Library, Vol. XXI.)

RADOCSAY, DÉNES: "Gótikus magyar címereslevelek" [Gothic Hungarian Letters Patent]. *Művészettörténeti Értesítő*, 1957, pp. 271–294. – "Gotische Wappenbilder auf ungarischen Adelsbriefen." *Acta Historiae Artium Academiae Scientiarum Hungaricae*, 1958, pp. 317–358. – "Gotische Wappenbilder auf ungarischen Adelsbriefen. 2." *Acta Historiae Artium Academiae Scientiarum Hungaricae*, 1964, pp. 57–68.

REIMAN, GEORG–BÜTTNER, HORST: *Mittelalterliche Buchmalerei in Sammlungen volksdemokratischer Länder.* Leipzig, 1961.

SABÓL, EUGEN: *Z dejin kódexov a miniatúr na Slovensku.* Martin, 1955.

SALMI, MARIO: *La miniatura italiana.* Milan, 1956.

SOLTÉSZ, ELIZABETH: "A Széchényi Könyvtár legszebb illuminált olaszországi ősnyomtatványai" [The Finest Illuminated Italian Incunabula of the National Széchényi Library]. *Az Országos Széchényi Könyvtár Évkönyve* [Year-book of the National Széchényi Library], 1957, pp. 140–141. – "Blutfogel Boldizsár miniator" [The Miniaturist Balthasar Blutfogel]. *Magyar Könyvszemle*, 1957, pp. 247–259.

SUIDA, WILHELM: *Österreichs Malerei in der Zeit Erzherzogs Ernst des Eisernen und König Albrecht II.* Vienna, 1926. – "Beiträge zur österreichischen Kunst der Spätgotik." *Belvedere*, 1927, pp. 72–75.

SWARZENSKI, GEORG: *Salzburger Malerei.* Leipzig, 1913, pp. 72–79.

SZÁNTÓ, TIBOR: "Ein grosser Schreibkünstler des XVI. Jahrhunderts." *Gutenberg-Jahrbuch*, 1963, pp. 37–40.

SZIGETI, KILIÁN: "A Mátyás-graduale eredetének kérdése" [On the Origin of King Matthias's Gradual]. *Magyar Könyvszemle*, 1963, No. 4, pp. 327–332.

UNTERKIRCHER, FRANZ: *Inventar der illuminierten Handschriften. Inkunabeln und Frühdrucke der Österreichischen Nationalbibliothek.* Part I. Vienna, 1957.

VAYER, LAJOS: *A rajzművészet mesterei. A Szépművészeti Múzeum régi külföldi rajzgyűjteményének legszebb lapjai.* Budapest, 1957, p. 19, No. 4. – *Master Drawings from the Collection of the Budapest Museum of Fine Arts (14th–18th Centuries).* New York–Amsterdam–London, 1964. – *Chefs-d'œuvre du dessin de la collection du Musée des Beaux-Arts de Budapest (XIVe–XVIIIe siècles).* Budapest, 1957. – *Meisterzeichnungen aus der Sammlung des Museums der Bildenden Künste in Budapest (14.–18. Jahrhundert).* Berlin, 1957. – *Masolino és Róma. Mecénás és művész a reneszánsz kezdetén* [Masolino and Rome. Patron and Artist in the Early Renaissance]. Budapest, 1962.

WITTGENS, F.: "Il Miniatore Francesco da Castello." *La Bibliofilia* XXXIX, pp. 7–8.

LIST OF MANUSCRIPTS, LETTERS PATENT AND INCUNABULA MENTIONED IN THE VOLUME

1 *The Szelepchényi Evangelistary*
11th century. 285 × 200 mm. Nitra, Capitular Archives 118

2 *Expositiones in Cantica Canticorum* (the manuscript of Bernard of Perugia)
12th century. 240 × 165 mm. Esztergom, FK Ms. II. 3

3 *The Pray Manuscript*
12th century. 235 × 150 mm. Budapest, OSZK MNY 1

4 *The Anonymus Gesta*
13th century. 240 × 170 mm. Budapest, OSZK Clmae 403

5 *Gradual*
Before 1334. 437 × 286 mm. Budapest, EK Cod. lat. 34 (formerly A. 102)

6 *Gradual*
Before 1334. 280 × 210 mm. Budapest, EK Cod. lat. 35 (formerly A. 103)

7 *Gradual*
About 1340. 472 × 294 mm. Budapest, EK Cod. lat. 123 (formerly A. 110)

8 *Missal*
About 1340. 336 × 237 mm. Budapest, OSZK Clmae 94

9 *Missal*
About 1340. 257 × 190 mm. Budapest, OSZK Clmae 435

10 *Missal*
About 1340. 315 × 223 mm. Budapest, OSZK Clmae 220

11 *Missal*
1341. 304 × 212 mm. Budapest, OSZK Clmae 214

12 *Missal*
Second half of the 14th century. 344 × 265 mm. Budapest, OSZK Clmae 215

13 *The Ganois Bible* (the manuscript of Wenceslas Ganois)
Second half of the 14th century. 345 × 248 mm. Budapest, OSZK Clmae 78

14 *Missal* (the manuscript of Stephanus Galsó of Sopron)
1363. 323 × 231 mm. Budapest, OSZK Clmae 91

15 *The Illuminated Chronicle*
Before 1370. 303 × 210 mm. Budapest, OSZK Clmae 404

16 *Missal*
Before 1389. 240 × 165 mm. Budapest, OSZK Clmae 395

17 *Breviary*
About 1390. 222 × 155 mm. Budapest, EK Cod. lat. 36

18 *Missal*
1394. 290 × 190 mm. Eger, Archiepiscopal Library, U 2. VI. 5

19 *Missal*
About 1403. 335 × 238 mm. Budapest, OSZK Clmae 216

20 *Ceremonial Book of the Goldsmiths' Guild of Vác*
1423. 399 × 309 mm. Budapest, OSZK Clmae 377

21 *The Pálóczy Missal* (manuscript of Georgius Pálóczy)
Between 1423 and 1439. 331 × 240 mm. Budapest, OSZK Clmae 359

22 *Antiphonary* (Georgius Pálóczy's manuscript)
Between 1423 and 1439. 480 × 350 mm. Esztergom, FK

23 *Missal*
About 1426. 354 × 269 mm. Budapest, OSZK Clmae 218

24 *Folio of a Missal*
About 1430. 313 × 227 mm. Budapest, Museum of Fine Arts, Graphic Art Department, No. 1938–3287

25 *Minute-Book of the Town of Selmecbánya*
1432. Paper. 410 × 280 mm. Budapest, Hungarian National Museum, Historical Department, No. 61. 54c

26 *Historia Troyana*
Between 1414 and 1434. 375 × 273 mm. Vienna, National Library Cod. Vindob. 2773

27 *Dionysius of Kistárkány's Letters Patent*
1434. 78 × 58 mm. Budapest, National Archives Dipl. 130.000

28 *The Victorinus Corvina Manuscript* (earlier in possession of Johannes Vitéz)
Before 1462. 303 × 204 mm. Budapest, OSZK Clmae 370

29 *Folio of an Antiphonary*
Second half of the 15th century. 604×390 mm. Budapest, Museum of Fine Arts, Graphic Art Department No. 1940–3515

30 *Missal*
Second half of the 15th century, *c.* 1480. 375×275 mm. Esztergom, FK Mss. I. 20

31 *Trapezuntius: Compendium grammaticae* (Corvina manuscript)
After 1470. 298×196 mm. Budapest, OSZK Clmae 428

32 *The Kálmáncsehi Breviary*
About 1481. 302×225 mm. Budapest, OSZK Clmae 446

33 *The Kálmáncsehi Missal*
Between 1481 and 1492. 231×163 mm. Zagreb, Archiepiscopal Library MR 355

34 *The Filipecz Pontifical* (Johannes Filipecz's manuscript)
Between 1476 and 1490. 343×240 mm. Esztergom, FK Ms. 26

35 *Trapezuntius: Rhetorica* (Corvina manuscript)
Between 1480 and 1490. 366×273 mm. Budapest, OSZK Clmae 281

36 *The Nagylucse Psalter* (the manuscript of Urbanus Dóczi de Nagylucse)
Between 1480 and 1498. 261×162 mm. Budapest, OSZK Clmae 369

37 *The Cyprianus Corvina Manuscript*
About 1470. 327×230 mm. Budapest, OSZK Clmae 529

38 *Breviary* (manuscript of Stephanus Nagylaki)
1489. 148×107 mm. Budapest, OSZK Clmae 343

39 *Prayer Book of Benigna Magyar, Wife of Pál Kinizsi* (Festetics manuscript)
Before 1494. 150×110 mm. Budapest, OSZK MNY 73

40 *Fragment of Antiphonary*
About 1490–1500. 556×360 mm. Budapest, Museum of Fine Arts, Graphic Art Department No. 1940–3467

41 *Psalter*
About 1500. 440×312 mm. Esztergom, FK

42 *Letters Patent of the Town of Kassa*
1502. 127×117 mm. Košice, Town Archives

43 *Felix Petancius Ragusinus: Genealogia Turcorum imperatorum*
Before 1512. Scroll, 2170×395 mm. Budapest, OSZK Clmae 378

44 *Evangelistary and Benedictionary* (Pannonhalma manuscript)
Before 1515 and 1515–1516. 311×215 mm. Budapest, EK Cod. lat. 113

45 *Gradual* (the Kassa Gradual) Vols. I and II. 1518. Vol. I: 715×560 mm; Vol. II: 715×545 mm. Budapest, OSZK, Vol. I: Clmae 452; Vol. II: Clmae 172

46 *Gradual* (Erdődy-Bakócz manuscript) Vol. I
Between 1519–1525 and 1557. 760×605 mm. Esztergom, FK

47 *Missal* (Incunabulum)
Venice, 1498 (owned by Franciscus Perényi), illuminated after 1514, around 1522? 217×310 mm. Győr, Episcopal Library

48 *Writing Pattern Book* (for King Ferdinand)
1562. 246×675 mm. Vienna, National Library Cod. Ser. n. 2664

49 *Missal*
Printed in Venice, 1511 (owned by Johannes Chereődi), illuminated in 1592. Paper and parchment. 352×246 mm. Esztergom, FK

LIST OF REPRODUCTIONS

LIST OF FIGURES IN TEXT

LIST OF PLATES

I Christ on the Cross. *Pray Manuscript*, fol. 27 (Budapest, OSZK MNY 1)

II The Deposition. *Pray Manuscript*, fol. 27v (Budapest, OSZK MNY 1)

III The Entombment; Visit to the Sepulchre. *Pray Manuscript*, fol. 28 (Budapest, OSZK MNY 1)

IV Christ Enthroned with the Angel Holding the Instruments of Torture. *Pray Manuscript*, fol. 28v (Budapest, OSZK MNY 1)

V Initial *A*. *Gradual*, fol. 3v (Budapest, EK Cod. lat. 34)

VI Initial *A* and border decoration. *Missal*, fol. 9 (Budapest, OSZK Clmae 94)

VII Christ on the Cross; initial *T*. *Missal*, fol. 15 (Budapest, OSZK Clmae 435)

VIII Christ on the Cross. *Missal*, fol. 144v (Budapest, OSZK Clmae 220)

IX The Nativity in the initial *P*, and border decoration. *Missal*, fol. 20 (Budapest, OSZK Clmae 215)

X The Agony of Christ. *Missal*, fol. 178 (Budapest, OSZK Clmae 215)

XI Crucifixion. *Missal*, fol. 178v (Budapest, Clmae 215)

XII In initial *F*, a bishop; border decoration with King David. *Ganois Bible*, fol. 1 (Budapest, OSZK Clmae 78)

XIII Scene of the Magyar Conquest. *Illuminated Chronicle*, fol. 21 (Budapest, OSZK Clmae 404)

XIV Christ on the Cross, and border-frame decoration. *Missal*, fol. 84 (Budapest, OSZK Clmae 395)

XV In initial *B*, King David. *Breviary*, fol. 1 (Budapest, EK Cod. lat. 36)

XVI In initial *A*, King David, and border decoration. *Missal*, fol. 11 (Budapest, OSZK Clmae 216)

XVII In initial *T*, the Agony of Christ. *Pálóczy Missal*, fol. 91 (Budapest, OSZK Clmae 359)

XVIII In initial *S*, Virgin and Child, and border decoration. *Antiphonary*, fol. 47 (Esztergom, FK)

XIX In initial *A*, King David, and border decoration. *Missal*, fol. 9 (Budapest, OSZK Clmae 218)

XX Christ on the Cross. Folio of *Missal* (Budapest, Museum of Fine Arts, Graphic Art Department No. 1938–3287)

XXI Crucifixion. *Minute-Book of the Town of Selmecbánya* (Banská Štiavnica), fol. 2v (Budapest, Hungarian National Museum, Historical Department No. 61.54c)

XXII Martha. Folio of *Antiphonary* (Budapest, Museum of Fine Arts, Graphic Art Department No. 1940–3515)

XXIII Initial *T*, and border decoration. *Missal*, fol. 67 (Esztergom, FK Mss. I. 20)

XXIV In initial *B*, King David; border-frame decoration with the arms of Dominicus Kálmáncsehi; the Life of David. Title-page of the *Kálmáncsehi Breviary*, fol. 7 (Budapest, OSZK Clmae 446)

XXV In initial *A*, the Nativity; border-frame decoration with the arms of Dominicus Kálmáncsehi; the Life of the Virgin. *Kálmáncsehi Breviary*, fol. 88v (Budapest, OSZK Clmae 446)

XXVI In initial *A*, Saints; border-frame decoration with the arms of Dominicus Kálmáncsehi and the Entry into Jerusalem. *Kálmáncsehi Breviary*, fol. 169 (Budapest, OSZK Clmae 446)

XXVII In initial *O*, the Holy Trinity; border-frame decoration with the arms of Dominicus Kálmáncsehi. *Kálmáncsehi Breviary*, fol. 211v (Budapest, OSZK Clmae 446)

XXVIII In initial *S*, the figure of Dominicus Kálmáncsehi kneeling before an altar; border-frame decoration with Dominicus Kálmáncsehi's arms and the artist's name. *Kálmáncsehi Breviary*, fol. 215 (Budapest, OSZK Clmae 446)

XXIX In initial *U* (*V*), God shows the Celestial City of Jerusalem to St John the Apostle; border-frame decoration with Dominicus Kálmáncsehi's arms. Christ, accompanied by saints, consecrates the church. *Kálmáncsehi Breviary*, fol. 269v (Budapest, OSZK Clmae 446)

XXX Initial *H* with recumbent female figure (Anne?); border-frame decoration with the arms of Dominicus Kálmáncsehi; Dominicus Kálmáncsehi kneeling before the Virgin and Child; Wild-boar hunt. *Kálmáncsehi Breviary*, fol. 308 (Budapest, OSZK Clmae 446)

XXXI In initial *D*, the Prophet Zachariah; border decoration. *Kálmáncsehi Breviary*, fol. 351v (Budapest, OSZK Clmae 446)

XXXII In initial *P*, Confirmation; border-frame decoration with the arms of Johannes Filipecz on the title-page of the *Filipecz Pontifical*, fol. 8 (Esztergom, FK Ms. 26)

XXXIII Initial *C*, and border-frame decoration with the arms of Matthias Corvinus. Title-page of *Trapezuntius*: *Rhetorica* (Budapest, OSZK Clmae 281)

XXXIV Initial *B* and border-frame decoration with the arms of Urbanus Dóczi de Nagylucse. Title-page of the *Nagylucse Psalter*. (Budapest, OSZK Clmae 369)

XXXV Coloured gilt edge of a Corvina manuscript. *Cyprianus Corvina Manuscript* (Budapest, OSZK Clmae 529)

XXXVI Border-frame decoration with the arms of Pál Kinizsi. *Prayer Book of Benigna Magyar, Wife of Pál Kinizsi*, fol. f 2^r (Budapest, OSZK MNY 73)

XXXVII In initial *S*, King David, and border decoration: Temptation of the Hermit St Anthony and His Meeting with the Hermit St Paul. Fragment of *Antiphonary* (Budapest, Museum of Fine Arts, Graphic Art Department No. 1940–3467)

XXXVIII In initial *E*, the Nativity; border-frame decoration: the Apostle Matthew, and St Martin with the Beggar. Title-page of *Evangelistary* (Budapest, EK Cod. lat. 113)

XXXIX In initial *C*, Falling of the Manna. *Kassa Gradual*, Vol. I, fol. 238v (Budapest, OSZK Clmae 452)

XL In initial *D*, the Baptism of Christ. *Kassa Gradual*, Vol. II, fol. 169v (Budapest, OSZK Clmae 172)

XLI In initial *A*, King David; border-frame decoration with the arms of Simon Erdődy-Bakócz; God the Father and the Annunciation. Title-page of the *Erdődy-Bakócz Gradual* (Esztergom, FK)

XLII In initial *P*, the Nativity (drawing), and border-frame decoration with the arms of Simon Erdődy-Bakócz; Annunciation to the Shepherds; Fortitude, Prudence (?), the Evangelists Mark, Luke and John. *Erdődy-Bakócz Gradual*, fol. 11v (Esztergom, FK)

XLIII Initial *G* and border-frame decoration. *Missal*, incunabulum, fol. 200 (Győr, Episcopal Library)

XLIV The Dance of Death. Death carries off a bishop. *Missal*, incunabulum, fol. 218 (Győr, Episcopal Library)

XLV (On a separate sheet at the end of the book) Representations of Turkish sultans and viziers. The *Genealogia Turcorum imperatorum of Felix Petancius Ragusinus* (Budapest, OSZK Clmae 378)

COLOUR PLATES

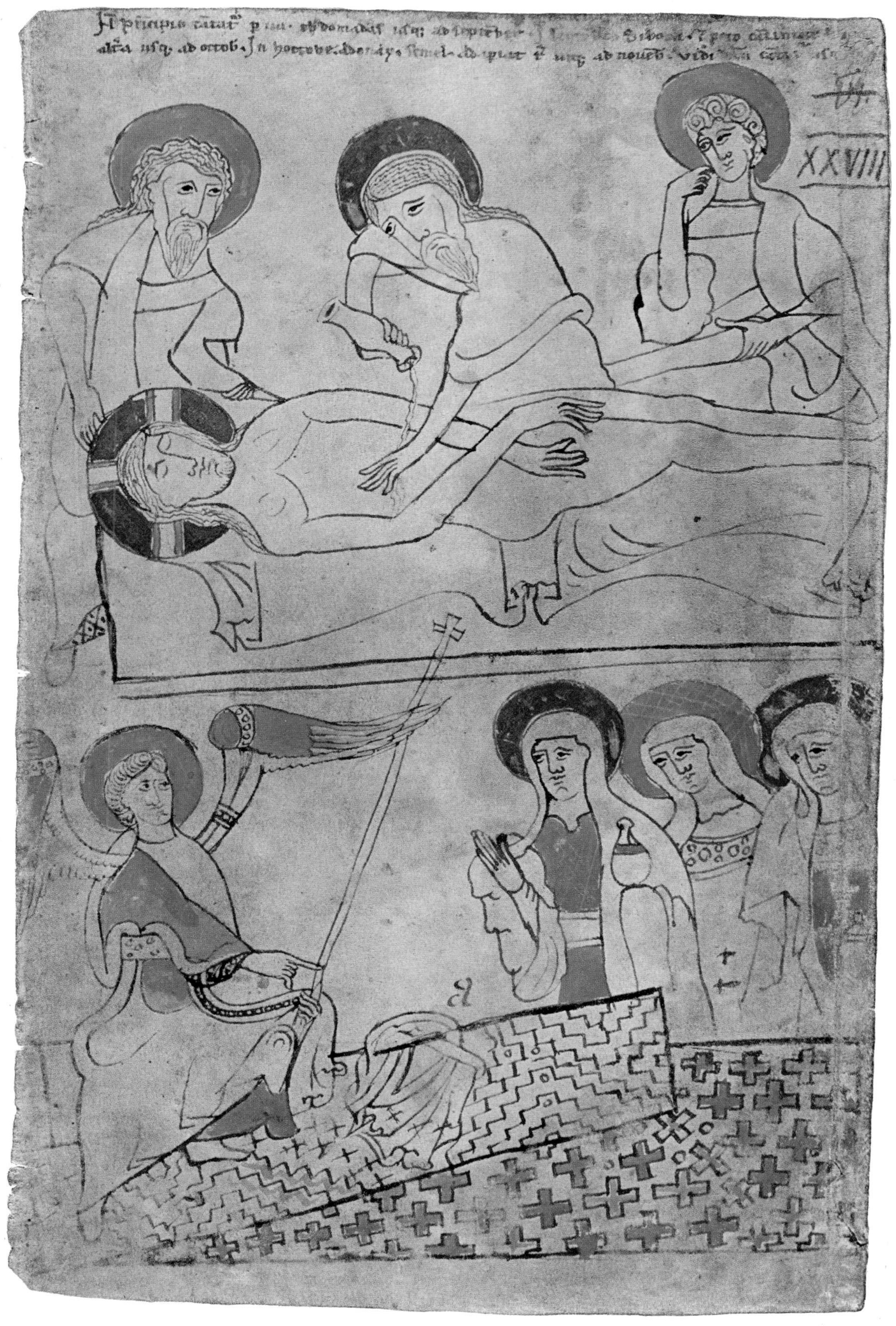
XXVIIII

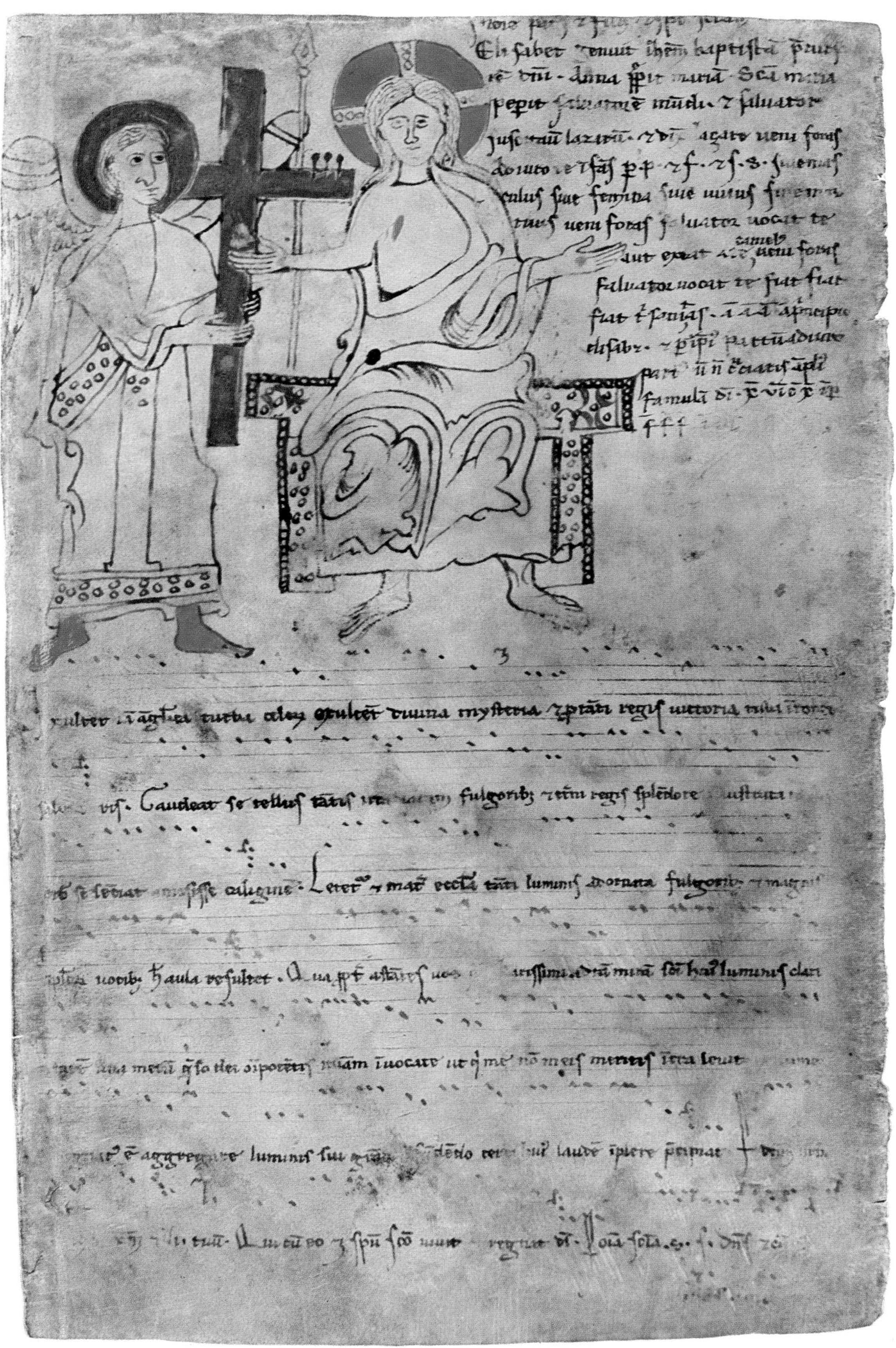

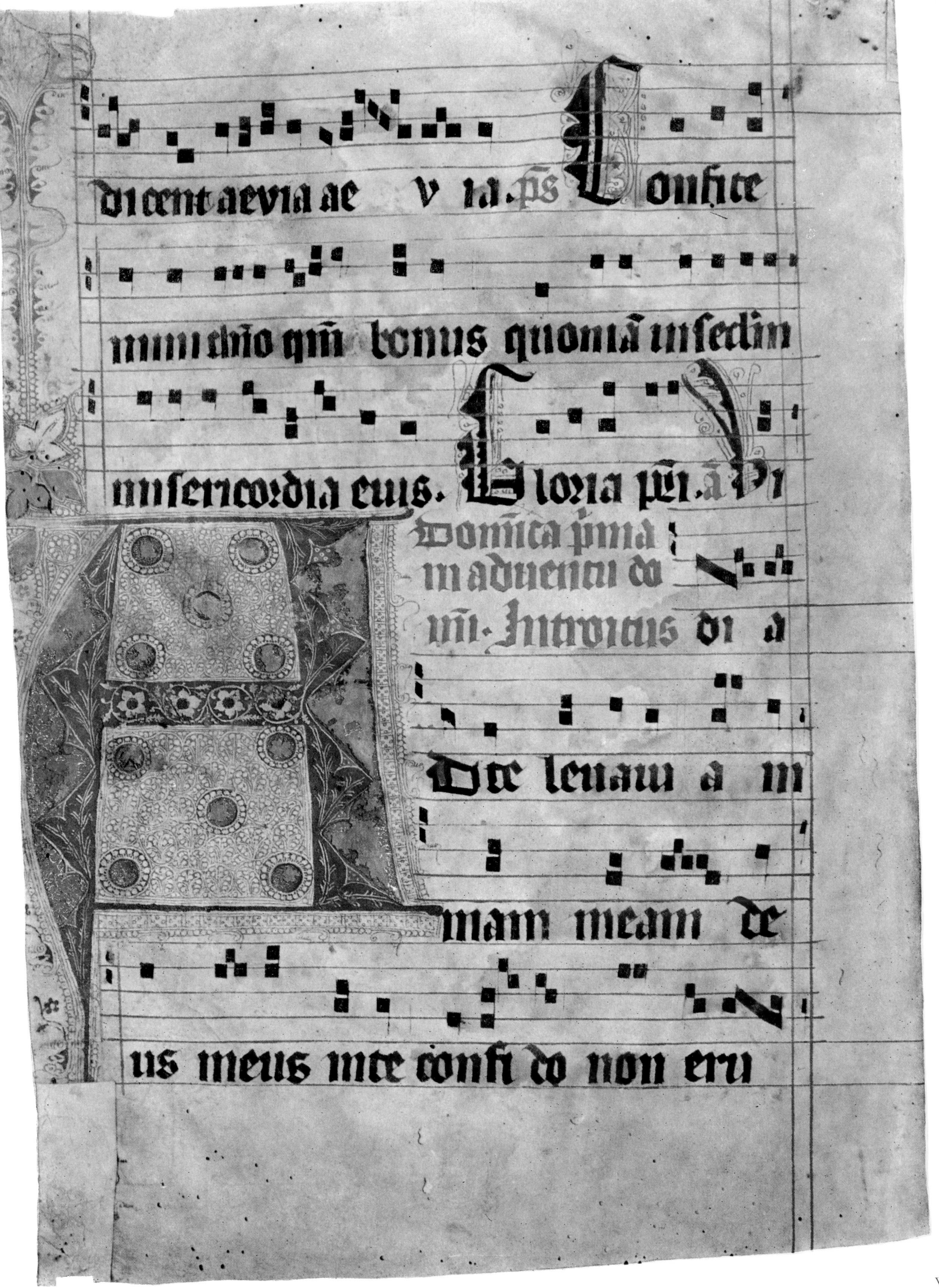

bonus
misericordia eius.
Gloria
Dominica prima in adventu domini.
Introitus
Ad te levavi a ni
mam meam de
us meus in te confi do non eru

V

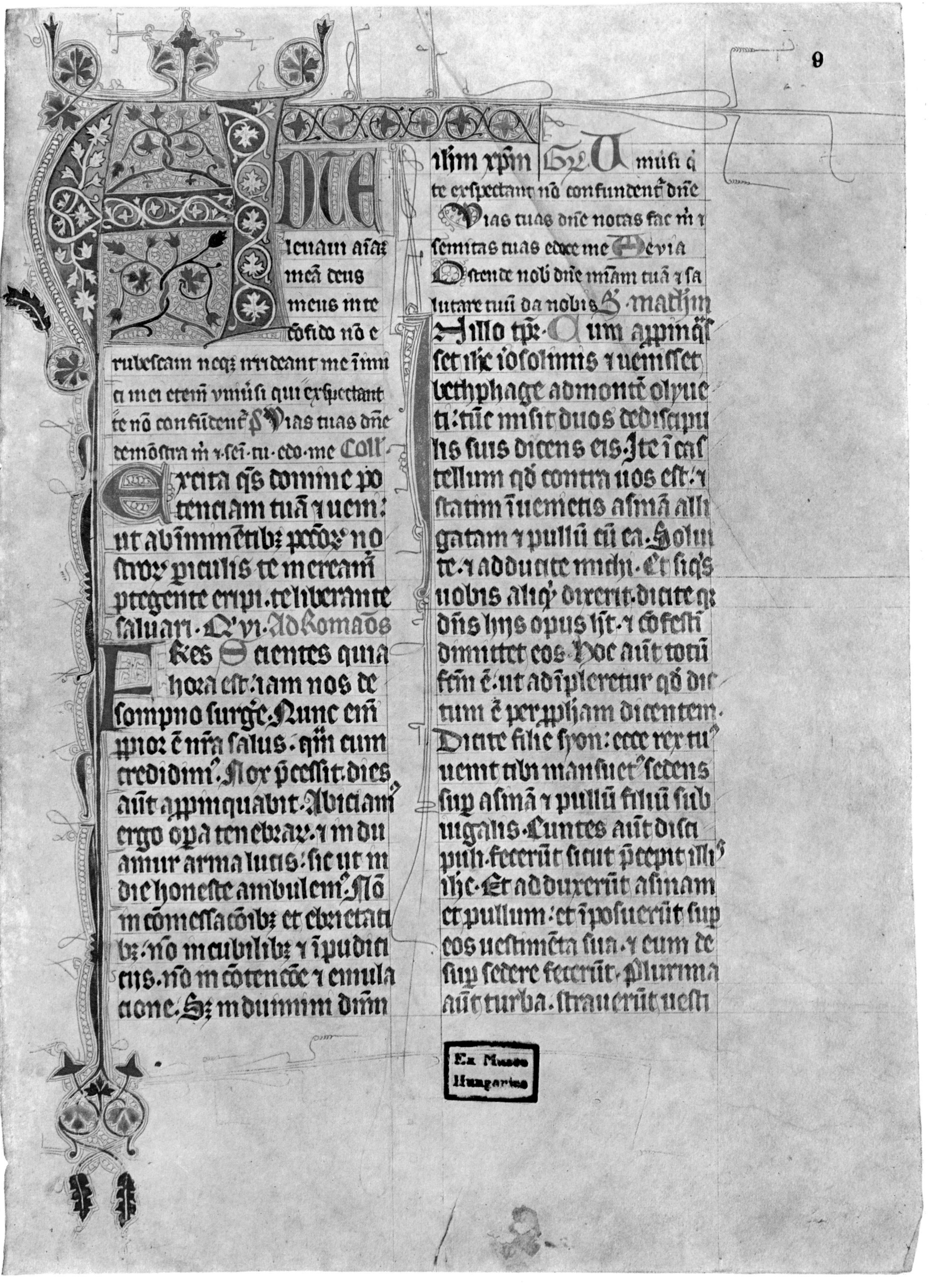

Ad te levavi animam meam deus meus in te confido non erubescam neque irrideant me inimici mei etenim universi qui exspectant te non confundentur. Ps. Vias tuas domine demonstra michi et semitas tuas edoce me. Coll. Excita quesumus domine potenciam tuam et veni: ut ab imminentibus peccatorum nostrorum periculis te mereamur protegente eripi, te liberante salvari. Qui vi. Ad Romanos. Fratres: Scientes quia hora est iam nos de sompno surgere. Nunc enim propior est nostra salus quam cum credidimus. Nox precessit, dies autem appropinquavit. Abiciamus ergo opera tenebrarum et induamur arma lucis: sicut in die honeste ambulemus. Non in comessacionibus et ebrietatibus, non in cubilibus et impudiciciis, non in contencione et emulacione. Sed induimini dominum Ihesum Christum. Gr. Universi qui te exspectant non confundentur domine. V. Vias tuas domine notas fac michi et semitas tuas edoce me. Alleluia. Ostende nobis domine misericordiam tuam et salutare tuum da nobis. S. Matheum. In illo tempore: Cum appropinquasset Ihesus Iherosolimis et venisset Bethphage ad montem Oliveti: tunc misit duos de discipulis suis dicens eis: Ite in castellum quod contra nos est, et statim invenietis asinam alligatam et pullum cum ea. Solvite et adducite michi. Et si quis vobis aliquid dixerit: dicite quia dominus hiis opus habet, et confestim dimittet eos. Hoc autem totum factum est ut adimpleretur quod dictum est per prophetam dicentem: Dicite filie Syon: ecce rex tuus venit tibi mansuetus sedens super asinam et pullum filium subiugalis. Euntes autem discipuli fecerunt sicut precepit illis Ihesus. Et adduxerunt asinam et pullum: et imposuerunt super eos vestimenta sua, et eum desuper sedere fecerunt. Plurima autem turba straverunt vesti-

INRI
15
Te igitur clementissime pater
per ihesum xpm filium tuum
dominum nostrum supplices
rogamus et petimus. uti accep
ta habeas et benedicas hec
dona ✠ hec mu✠nera:
hec sancta sacri✠ficia il
libata. In primis que tibi
offerimus pro ecclia tua sancta katholica. quam
pacificare. custodire. adunare et regere digneris
toto orbe terrarum. una cum famulo tuo papa

I·N·R·I·

uersi sunt pastores glorificantes et
laudantes dominum in omnibus que au
dierant et uiderant sicut dictum est
ad illos. off. Deus enim firmauit
orbem terre qui non commouebitur para
ta sedes tua deus extunc a seculo tu es.
Munera quesumus domine natiuitatis Secr
tis hodierne mysteriis apta pro
ueniant ut sicut homo genitus
idem refulsit deus sic nobis hec
terrena substancia conferat quod
diuinum est. Per eundem. Aliud secret.
Accipe quesumus domine munera dignanter
oblata et beate anastasie suffra
gantibus meritis ad nostre salutis
auxilium prouenire concede. Per.
prefatio Quia per incarnati. Commu
nicantes. com. Exulta satis filia
syon lauda filia ierusalem ecce rex tuus uenit
sanctus et saluator mundi. Complend.
Huius nos domine sacramenti
semper nouitas natalis instau
ret cuius natiuitas singularis
humanam repulit uetustatem.
Per. alia co. Sacrasti domine fam
iliam tuam muneribus sacris eius
que semper interuencione nos refo
ue cuius solempnia celebramus.
In die sancto. Per.
Puer natus est no
bis et filius datus
est nobis cuius
imperium super
humerum eius et uocabitur nomen
eius magni consilii angelus. Ps. Can
tate domino canticum nouum quia mirabilia fe.
Concede quesumus omnipotens deus or.
ut nos unigeniti tui
noua per carnem natiuitas liberet
quos sub peccati iugo uetusta
seruitus tenet. Per eundem. l. ysaie
Hec dicit dominus. Propter
hoc sciet populus meus nomen
meum in die illa quia ego ipse
qui loquebar ecce assum. Quam
pulchri super montes pedes annun
ciantis et predicantis pacem annun
ciantis bonum predicantis salutem
dicentis Syon regnabit deus tuus.
Vox speculatorum tuorum leuauerunt

TE·IGITUR

Frater Ambrosius tua mihi munuscula perferens detulit et suavissimas litteras, quae a principio amicitiarum fidem probatae iam fidei et veteris amicitiae praeferebant. Vera enim illa necessitudo est et Christi glutino copulata, quam non utilitas rei familiaris, non praesentia tantum corporum, non subdola et palpans adulatio, sed Dei timor et divinarum scripturarum studia conciliant. Legimus in veteribus historiis quosdam lustrasse provincias, novos adisse populos, maria transisse, ut eos quos ex libris noverant coram quoque viderent. Sic Pythagoras Memphiticos vates, sic Plato Aegyptum et Archytam Tarentinum eamque oram Italiae quae quondam Magna Graecia dicebatur laboriosissime peragravit, ut qui Athenis magister erat et potens cuiusque doctrinas Academiae gymnasia personabant, fieret peregrinus atque discipulus, malens aliena verecunde discere quam sua impudenter ingerere. Denique cum litteras quasi toto orbe fugientes persequitur, captus a piratis et venundatus etiam tyranno crudelissimo paruit, ductus captivus vinctus et servus; tamen quia philosophus maior ementem se fuit. Ad Titum Livium lacteo eloquentiae fonte manantem de ultimis Hispaniae Galliarumque finibus quosdam venisse nobiles legimus, et quos ad contemplationem sui Roma non traxerat, unius hominis fama perduxit. Habuit illa aetas inauditum omnibus saeculis celebrandumque miraculum, ut urbem tantam ingressi aliud extra urbem quaererent. Apollonius, sive ille magus ut vulgus loquitur, sive philosophus ut Pythagorici tradunt, intravit Persas, pertransivit Caucasum, Albanos, Scythas, Massagetas, opulentissima Indiae regna penetravit, et ad extremum latissimo Phison amne transmisso pervenit ad Brachmanas, ut Hiarcam in throno sedentem aureo et de Tantali fonte potantem inter paucos discipulos de natura, de moribus ac de cursu dierum et siderum audiret docentem. Inde per Elamitas, Babylonios, Chaldaeos, Medos, Assyrios, Parthos, Syros, Phoenices, Arabes, Palaestinos reversus ad Alexandriam perrexit Aethiopiam, ut gymnosophistas et famosissimam Solis mensam videret in sabulo. Invenit ille vir ubique quod disceret, et semper proficiens semper se melior fieret. Scripsit super hoc plenissime octo voluminibus Philostratus.

II

Quid loquar de saeculi hominibus, cum apostolus Paulus, vas electionis et magister gentium, qui de conscientia tanti in se hospitis loquebatur dicens: An experimentum quaeritis eius qui in me loquitur Christus? post Damascum Arabiamque lustratam ascendit Ierosolymam ut videret Petrum et mansit apud eum diebus quindecim. Hoc enim mysterio hebdomadis et ogdoadis futurus gentium praedicator instruendus erat. Rursum post annos quattuordecim assumpto Barnaba et Tito exposuit cum apostolis evangelium, ne forte in vacuum curreret aut cucurrisset. Habet nescio quid latentis energiae vivae vocis actus, et in aures discipuli de auctoris ore transfusa fortius sonat. Unde et Aeschines cum Rhodi exularet et legeretur illa Demosthenis oratio quam adversus eum habuerat, mirantibus cunctis atque laudantibus suspirans ait: Quid si ipsam audissetis bestiam sua verba resonantem?

III

Non hoc dico quod sit aliquid tale in me quod vel possis a me audire vel velis discere, sed quo ardor tuus et discendi studium etiam absque nobis per se probari debeat. Ingenium docile et sine doctore laudabile est. Non quid invenias, sed quid quaeras consideramus. Mollis cera et ad formandum facilis, etiam si artificis et plastae cessent manus, tamen virtute totum quicquid esse potest. Paulus apostolus ad pedes Gamalielis legem Moysi et prophetas didicisse se gloriatur, ut armatus spiritalibus telis postea diceret confidenter: Arma enim militiae nostrae non carnalia sunt, sed potentia Deo ad destructionem munitionum, consilia destruentes et omnem altitudinem extollentem se adversus scientiam Dei, et captivantes omnem intellectum ad obediendum Christo

Capituli Posoniensis 1633. Lit B.

INRI

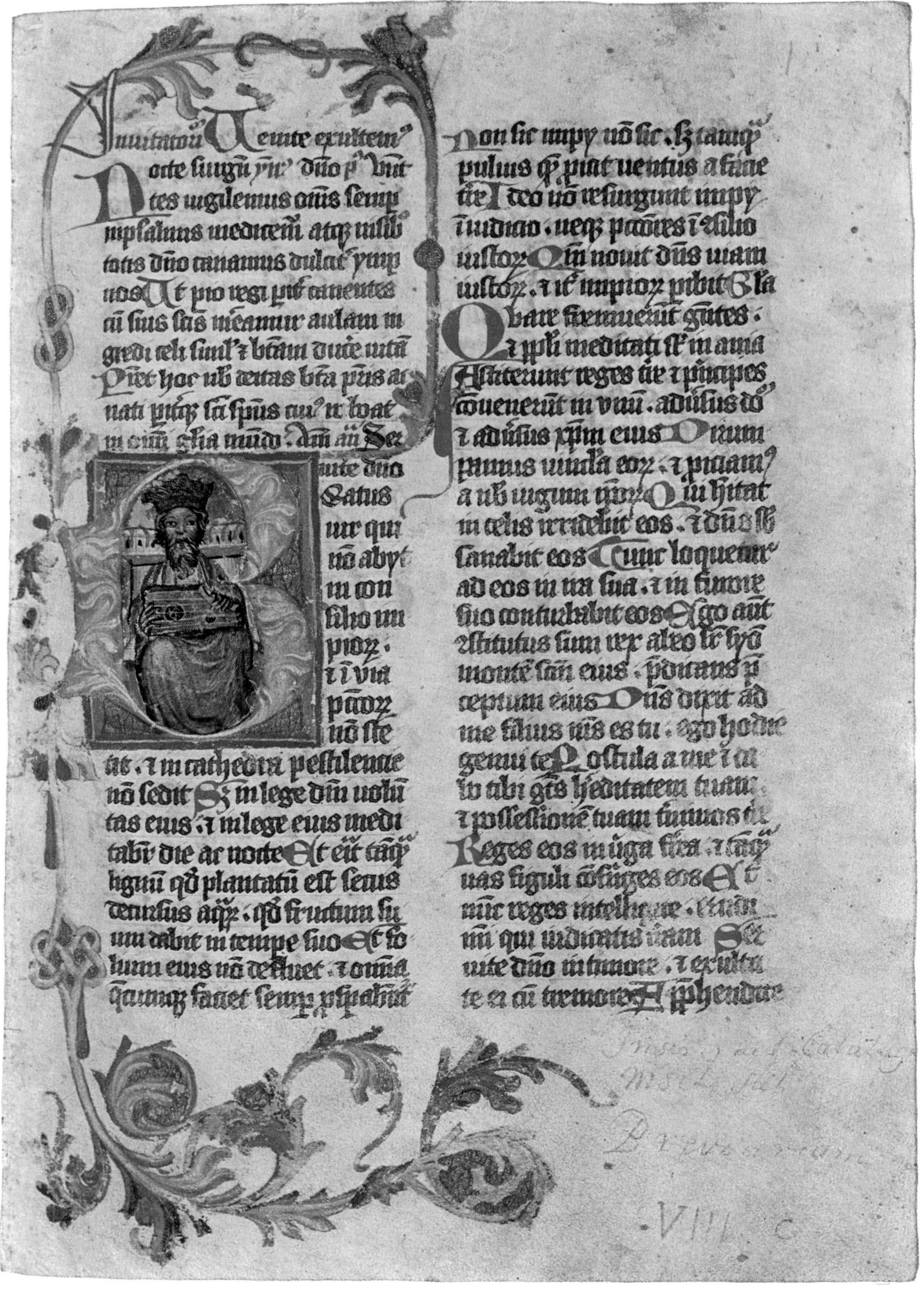

[A]d te levavi animam meam deus
meus in te confido non erubescam
neque irrideant me inimici mei
etenim universi qui te expectant
non confundentur. ps. Vias
tuas domine demonstra michi
et semitas tuas edoce me. Oratio
[E]xcita quesumus domine
potenciam tuam et veni.
ut ab imminentibus peccatorum nostrorum periculis. te mereamur protegente eripi. te liberante salvari. Qui vivis. Leccio e. b. p.
[F]ratres. a. Ad Romanos.
[S]cientes quia hora
est iam nos de sompno surgere.

Nunc enim propior est nostra
salus. quam cum credidimus.
Nox precessit dies autem appro-
pinquabit. Abiciamus ergo o-
pera tenebrarum. et induamur
arma lucis. ut in die honeste
ambulemus. Non in comessacionibus et ebrietatibus. non in
cubilibus et impudiciis. non in
contencione et emulacione. Sed induimini dominum ihesum christum. Gr.
[U]niversi qui te exspectant non
confundentur domine. V. Vias
tuas domine notas fac michi
et semitas tuas edoce me. Alleluia. versus. Ostende nobis
domine misericordiam tuam et salutare
tuum da nobis. Secundum Matheum.
[I]n illo tempore. Cum appropinquasset
ihesus iherosolimis et venisset bethphage ad montem oliveti. tunc
misit duos de discipulis suis
dicens eis. Ite in castellum
quod contra vos est. et statim
invenietis asinam alligatam
et pullum cum ea. Solvite
et adducite michi. Et si quis
vobis aliquid dixerit. dicite quia
dominus hiis opus habet.

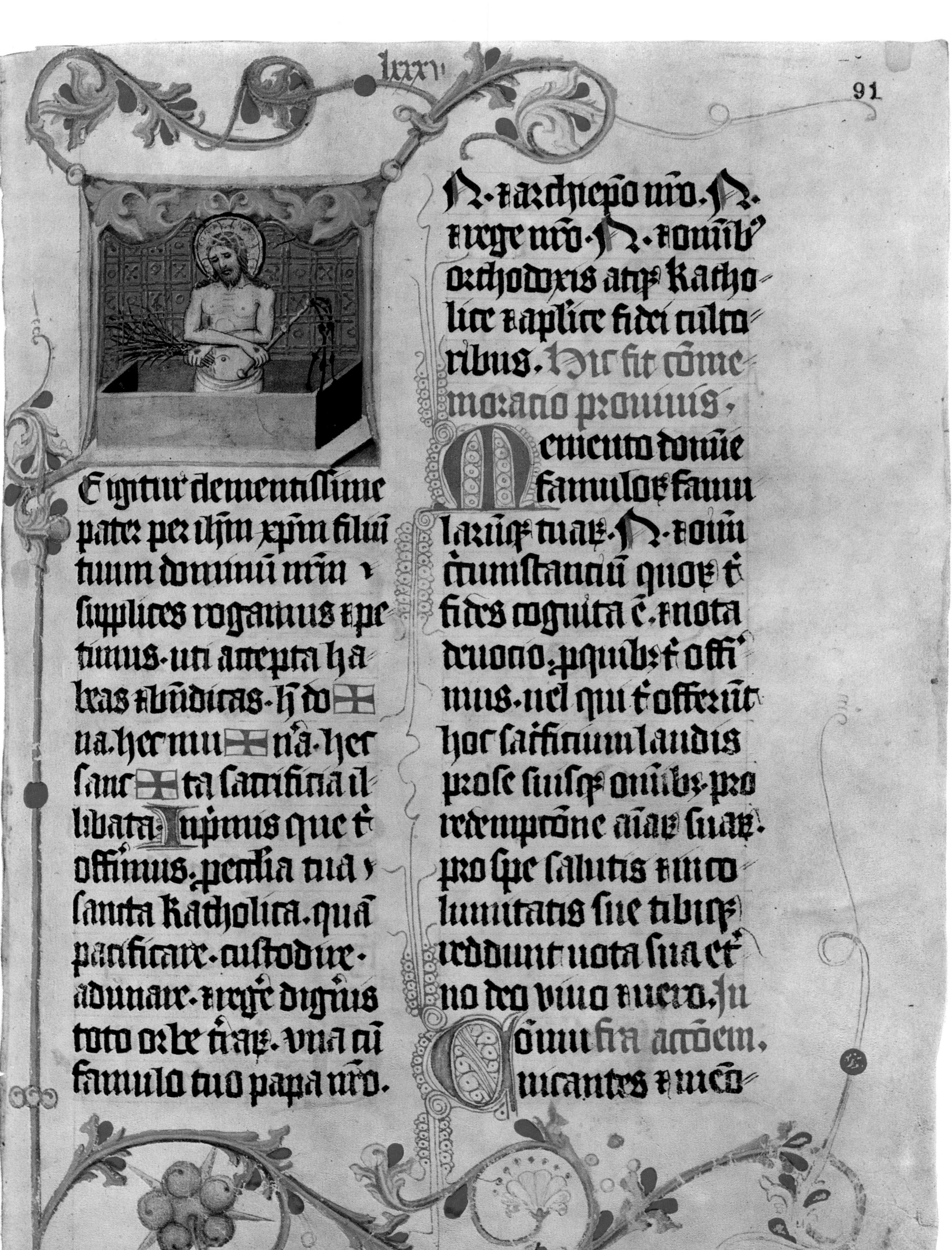

Te igitur clementissime
pater per ihesum christum filium
tuum dominum nostrum
supplices rogamus et pe
timus. uti accepta ha
beas et benedicas. hec do ✠
na. hec mu ✠ nera. hec
sanc ✠ ta sacrificia il
libata. In primis que tibi
offerimus. pro ecclesia tua
sancta katholica. quam
pacificare. custodire.
adunare. et regere digneris
toto orbe terrarum. una cum
famulo tuo papa nostro.

N. et archiepiscopo nostro. N.
et rege nostro. N. et omnibus
orthodoxis atque katho
lice et apostolice fidei culto
ribus. Hic fit comme
moracio pro uiuis.
Memento domine
famulorum famu
larumque tuarum. N. et omni
um circumstancium quorum tibi
fides cognita est et nota
deuocio. pro quibus tibi offeri
mus. uel qui tibi offerunt
hoc sacrificium laudis
pro se suisque omnibus. pro
redempcione animarum suarum.
pro spe salutis et inco
lumitatis sue tibique
reddunt uota sua eter
no deo uiuo et uero. In
Communi fra accionem.
cantes et memo

Maria v̄go
intercede p to
to mundo quia genuisti rege
orbis · p Tanď
rerum creator miserere poplo
198
47

9

Ad te leuaui animam meam de
us meus in te confido non erubes
cam neque irrideant me inimici
mei etenim uniuersi qui te exspe
tant non confundentur ps Vias
tuas domine demonstra michi et semita
tuas edoce me · Oratio sequitur
Excita domine potentiam
tuam et veni ut ab im
minentibus peccatorum nostrorum
periculis te mereamur protege
te eripi te liberante saluari · Qui
Fratres · Lc · e · b pauli apostoli
Scientes quia Ad romanos
hora est iam nos de sompno sur
gere · Nunc enim propior est nostra
salus quam cum credidimus
Nox precessit · dies autem appropin
quabit · Abiciamus ergo opera
tenebrarum · et induamur arma
lucis · sicut in die honeste ambu
lemus · Non in comessationibus
et ebrietatibus · non in cubilibus
et impudicitiis · non in contenti
one · et emulacione · sed induimini
dominum ihesum christum · Gr · Universi
qui te exspectant non confundentur
domine · V · Vias tuas domine notas
fac michi et semitas tuas edoce
me · Alleluia · V · Ostende nobis domine mi
sericordiam tuam et salutare tuum
da nobis · Secundum matheum ·
In illo t · Cum appropinquasset ihesus
ierosolimis · et venisset bethpha
ge ad montem oliveti · tunc mi
sit duos discipulos dicens eis ·
Ite in castellum quod contra
vos est · et statim invenietis asi
nam alligatam · et pullum cum
ea · Solvite et adducite michi · Et
si quis vobis aliquid dixerit
dicite quia dominus hiis opus habet ·
et confestim dimittet eos · Hoc
autem factum est · ut adimpleretur
quod dictum est per prophetam dicen
tem · Dicite filie syon ecce rex tuus
venit tibi mansuetus · et sedens
super asinam et pullum filium sub

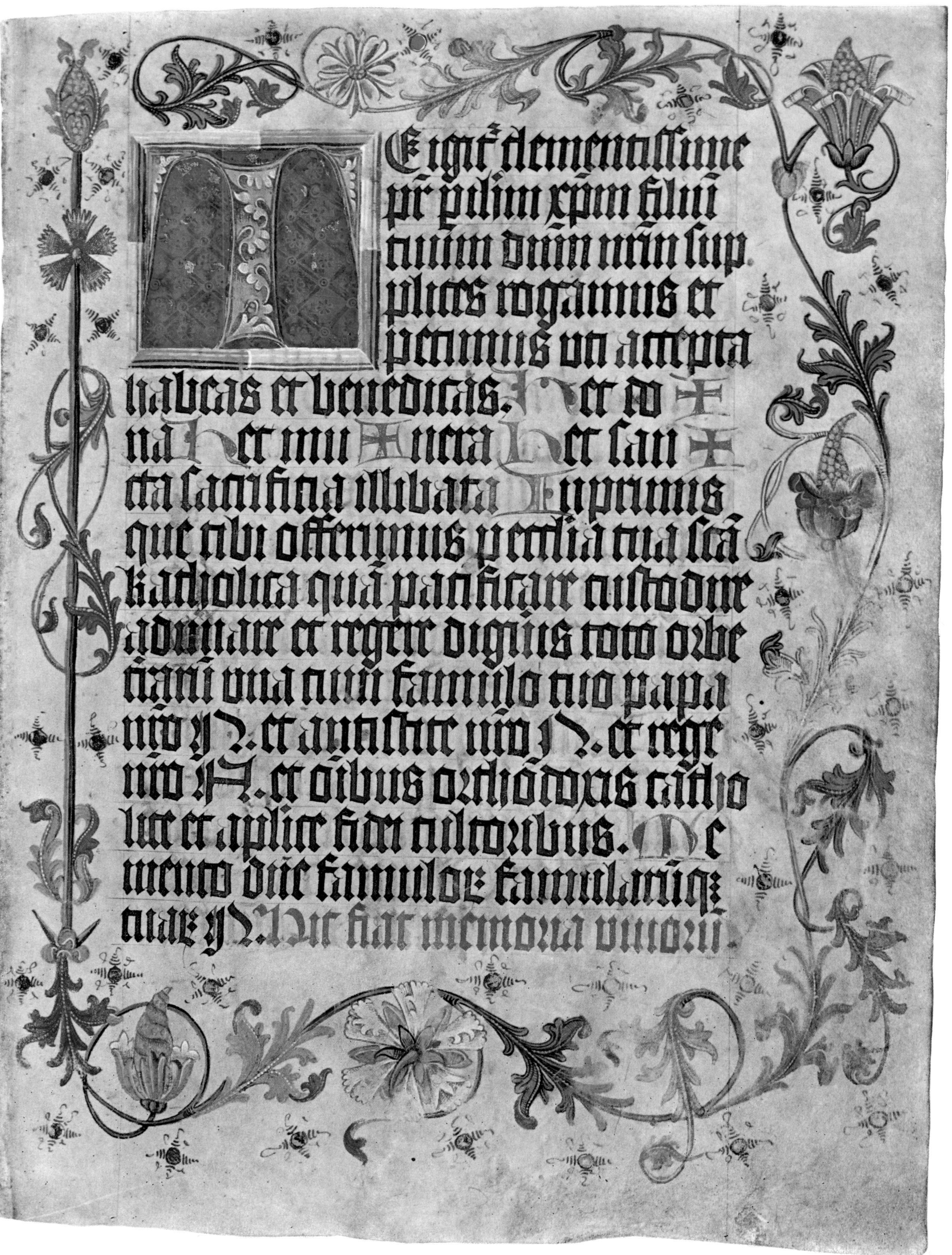
Te igitur clementissime
pater per ihesum christum filium
tuum dominum nostrum sup
plices rogamus et
petimus uti accepta
habeas et benedicas. Hec do +
na. Hec mu + nera. Hec san +
cta sacrificia illibata. In primis
que tibi offerimus pro ecclesia tua sancta
katholica quam pacificare custodire
adunare et regere digneris toto orbe
terrarum una cum famulo tuo papa
nostro N. et antistite nostro N. et rege
nostro N. et omnibus orthodoxis atque catho
lice et apostolice fidei cultoribus. Me
mento domine famulorum famularumque
tuarum N. Hic fiat memoria vivorum

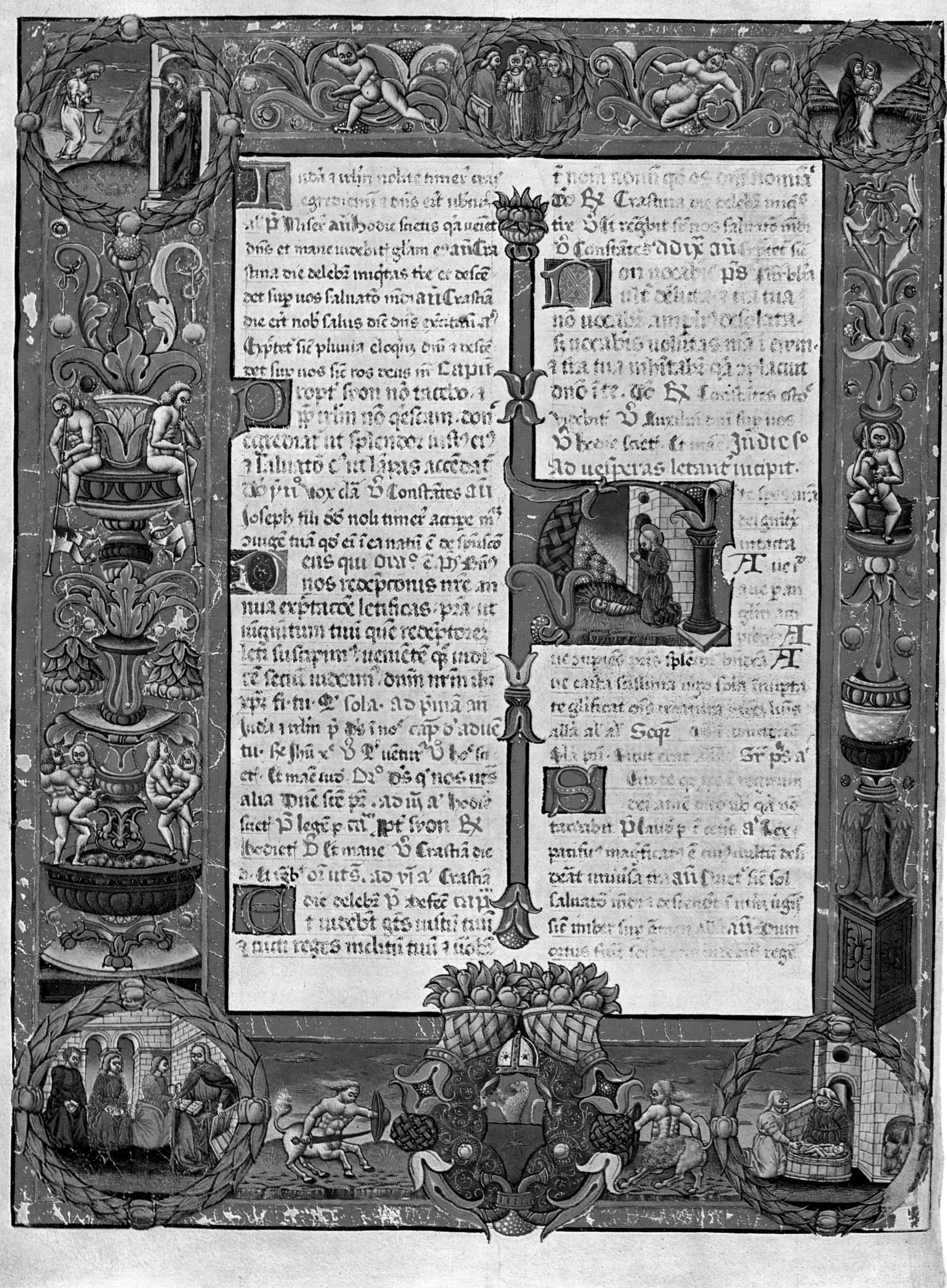

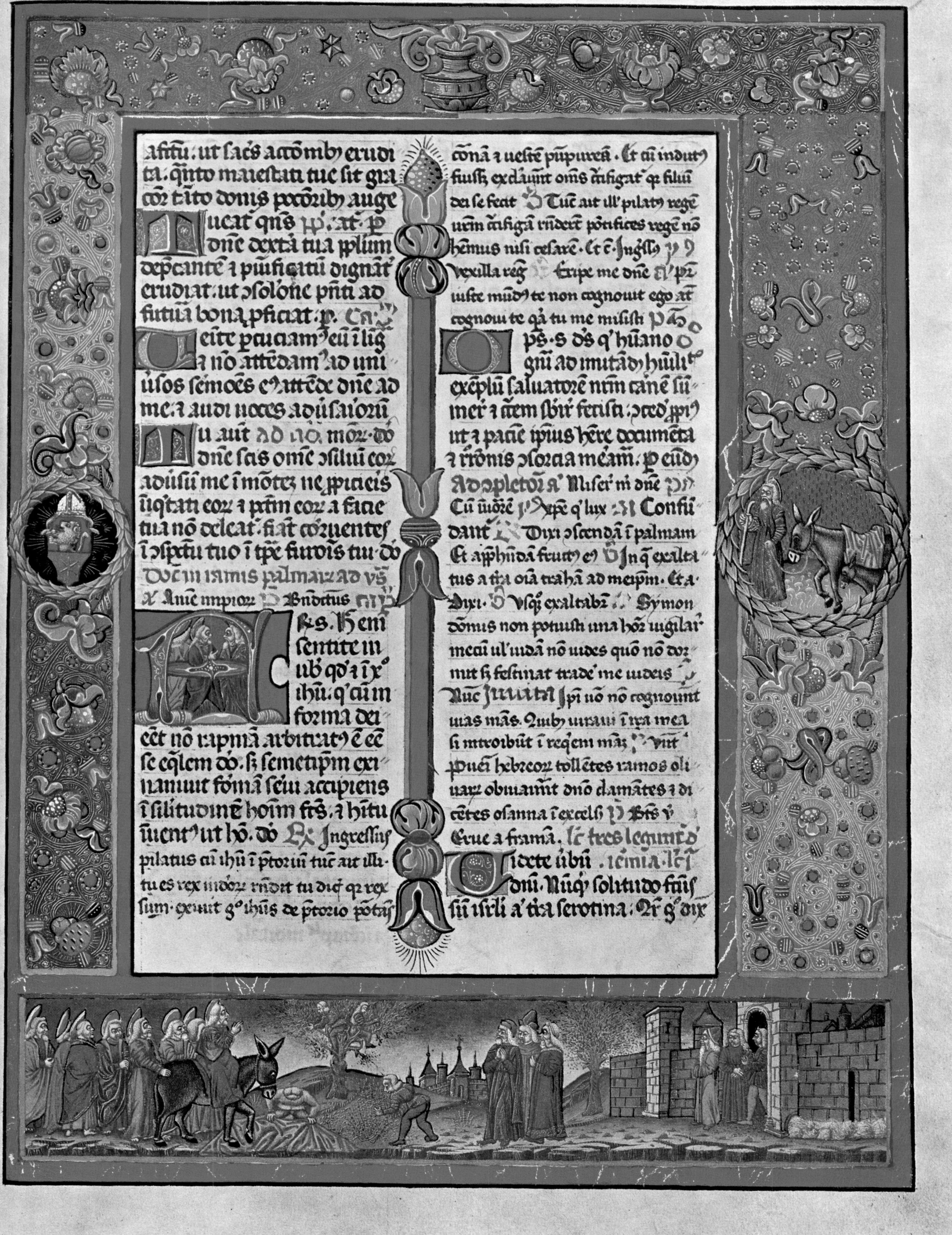

astitu. ut sac(r)is actoibus erudi
ta. q(ua)nto maiestati tue sit gra
cior: tanto donis pocioribus auge
scat q(ui)s p(er). ait. p
Adiuvet q(ue)s
dne dextera tua p(o)p(u)lum
depcantem: i purificatum dignant(er)
erudiat: ut (con)solone p(re)nti ad
futura bona p(ro)ficiat. p. Tra
Venite mittam(us) lign(um) i(n) pane eius ... et
ra(dam)us eum de t(er)ra viven(tium) ...
... Tu aut(em) d(omi)ne sabaoth ...
... Tu aut(em) dne scis omne (con)siliu(m) eor(um)
aduersu(m) me i(n) morte(m) ne p(ro)picieris
iniq(ui)tati eor(um) ...
Dne in ramis palmarum
... Benedictus ...
Hoc enim sentite in
vobis q(uo)d i(n) x(ris)to
ihu. q(ui) cu(m) in
forma dei
ect no(n) rapina(m) arbitrat(us) e(st) ee
se eq(ua)lem deo. s(ed) semetip(su)m exi
naniuit forma(m) servi accipiens
i(n) silitudine(m) hoim f(a)c(tu)s. et habitu
inuent(us) ut ho. Ev. Ingressus
pilatus cu(m) ihu i(n) p(re)toriu(m) tu(n)c ait illi.
tu es rex iudeor(um) r(espo)ndit tu dic(is) q(uia) rex
sum. exiuit (er)go ihus de p(re)torio portans

corona(m) et veste(m) purpurea(m). Et cu(m) induti
fuiss(et) exclamau(er)u(n)t oms crucifigat(ur) q(ui)a filiu(m)
dei se fecit Tu(n)c ait ill(is) pilat(us) rege(m)
u(est)r(u)m crucifiga(m) r(espo)nder(un)t pontifices rege(m) no(n)
habemus nisi cesare(m). Et c(etera). Ingress(us) ...
Vexilla reg(is) Eripe me dne ... P(at)er
iuste mu(n)d(us) te non cognouit ego aut(em)
cognoui te q(ui)a tu me misisti ...
Omnipotens s(empiterne) d(eu)s q(ui) hu(m)ano
ge(ner)i ad imita(n)d(um) humili(tatis)
exemplu(m) saluatore(m) n(ost)r(u)m carne(m) su(m)
mere et cruce(m) subire fecisti: (con)cede p(ro)picius
ut et pacie(n)c(ie) ip(s)ius h(ab)ere documenta
et resurrectionis (con)sorcia mereamur. P(er) eund(em)
Ad (com)pletoriu(m) a(ntiphona). Miserere mi dne ...
Cu(m) inuocare(m) ... Ipse q(ui) lux ... Confi
dant ... Dixi ascenda(m) i(n) palmam
Et app(re)henda(m) fruct(us) ei(us) ... In q(uo) exalta
tus a t(er)ra o(mn)ia traha(m) ad meip(su)m. Et a
Dixi ... Usq(ue) exaltabi(tur) ... Symon
dormis non potuisti una hora vigilar(e)
mecu(m) u(el) iuda(m) no(n) vides quo(modo) no(n) dor
mit s(ed) festinat trade(re) me iudeis ...
Nu(n)c iudicatur ... Ipsi u(er)o no(n) cognouerunt
vias meas. Quib(us) iuraui i(n) ira mea
si introibu(n)t i(n) requiem mea(m) ... Inv(itatorium)
Pueri hebreor(um) tolle(n)tes ramos oli
uar(um) obuiaueru(n)t dno clamantes et di
ce(n)tes osanna i(n) excelsis ... Ps(alm)us
Erue a framea. Lc(ciones) tres legu(n)t(ur) d(e)
Videte uiui ... ieremia. Lc(cio) i
Dni. Nu(n)q(ui)d solitudo fact(us)
su(m) isr(ae)li a(ut) t(er)ra serotina. Qu(are) (er)go dix(erunt)

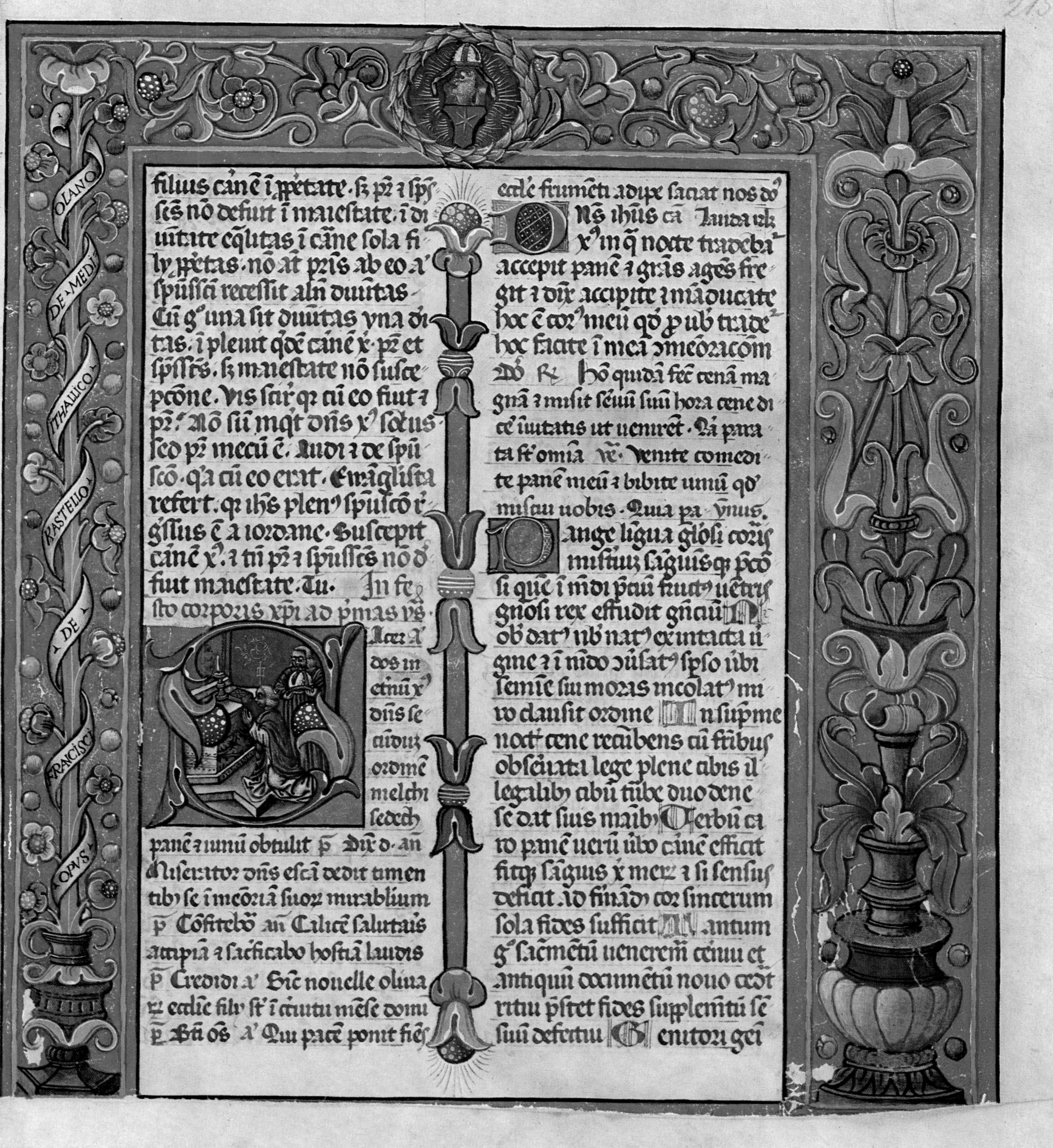
OPUS
FRACISCI
DE
CASTELLO
ITHALLICO
DE·MEDI
OLANO

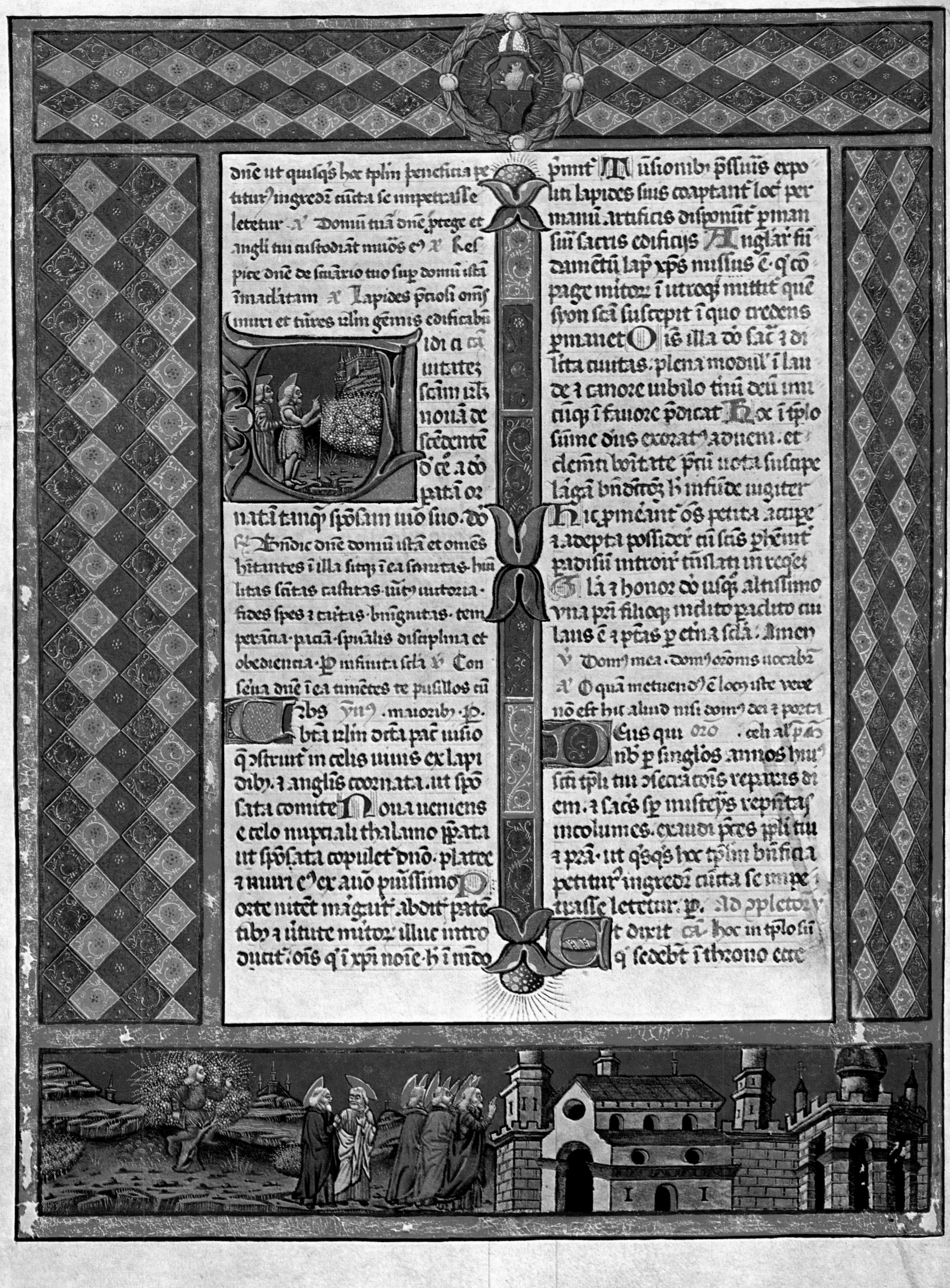

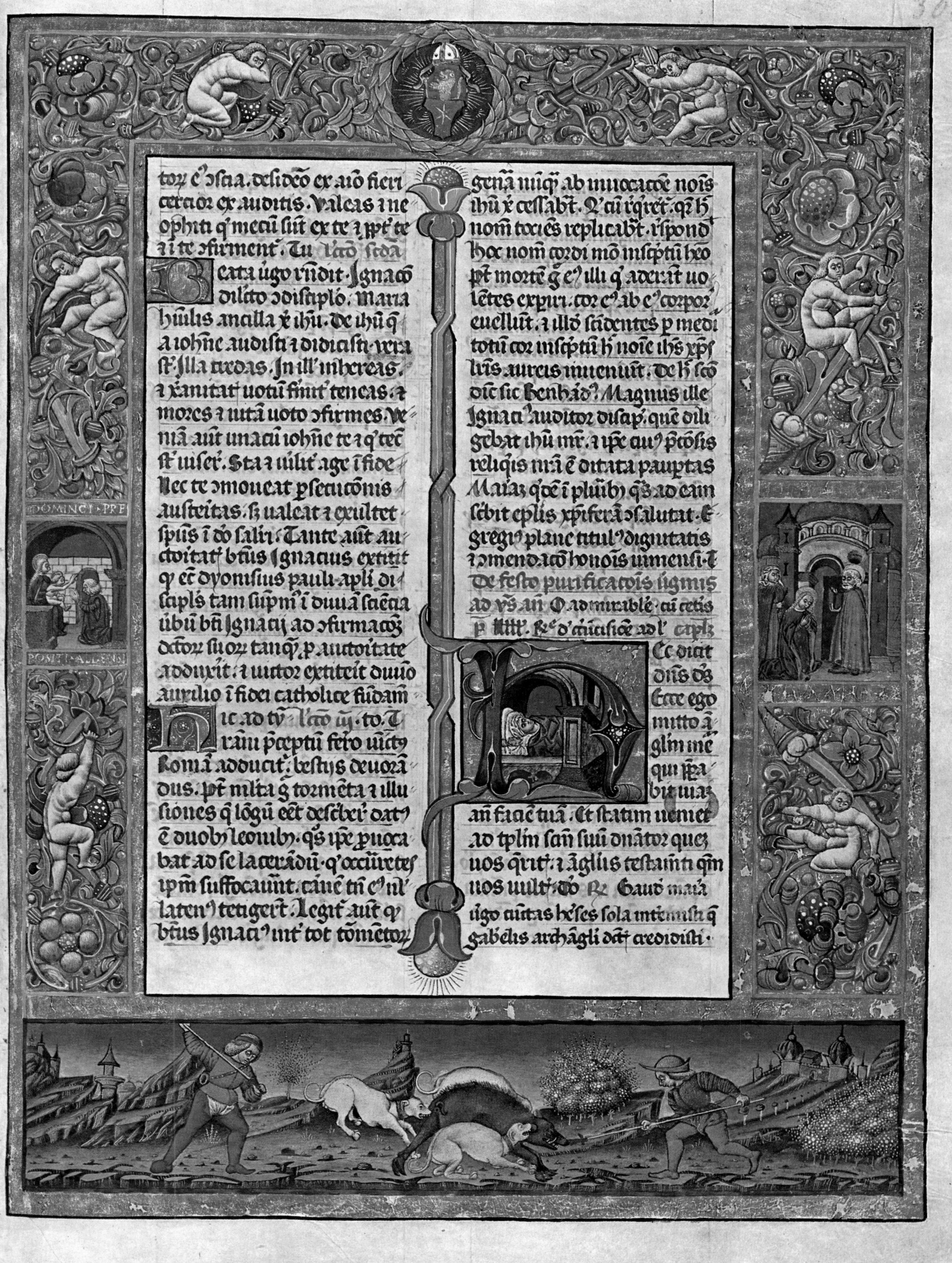

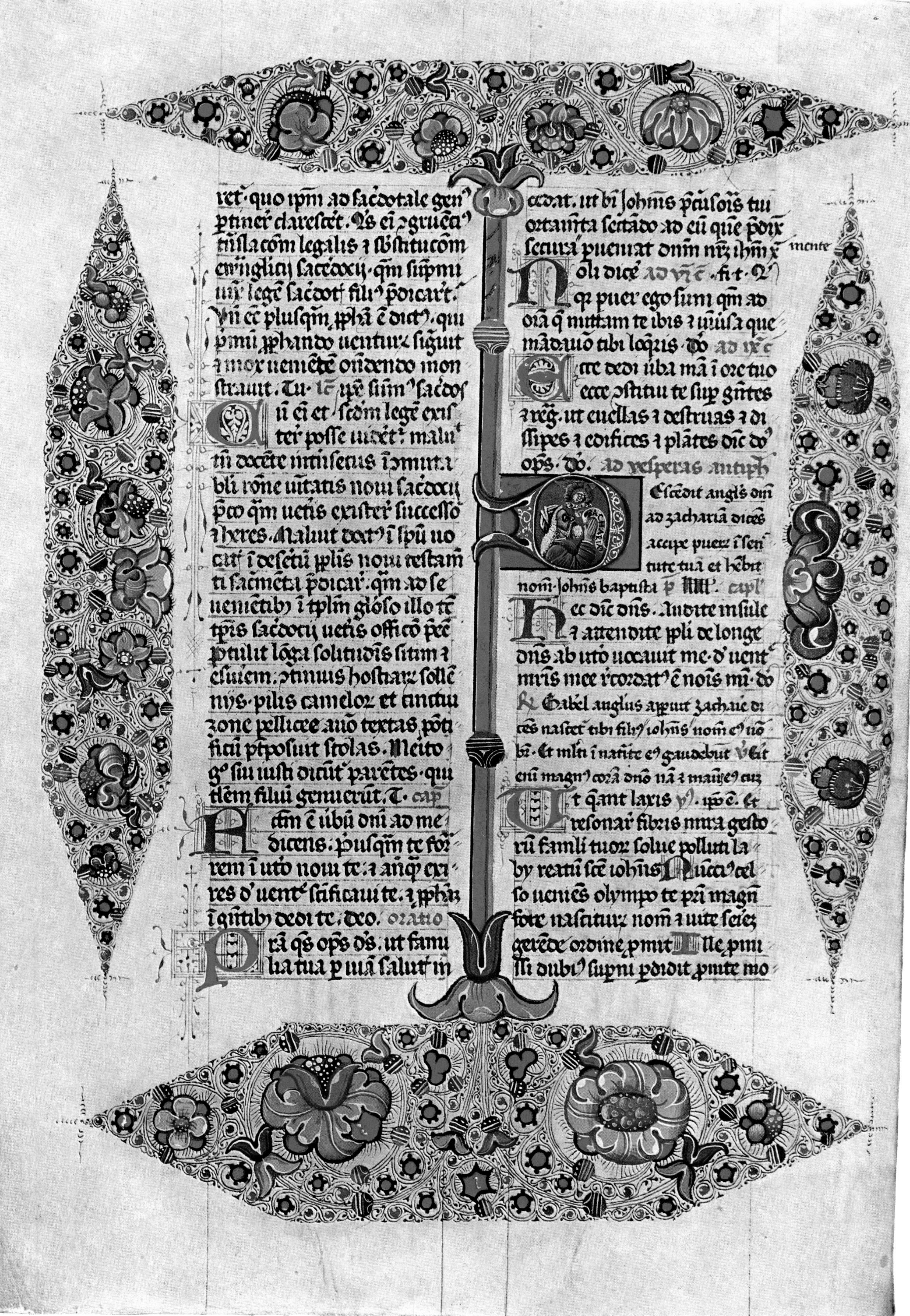
ret· quo ipm ad sacdotale gen
ptiner claresceret. Vs ei 9gruēca
tiisla cōm legalis 7 9stitucōm
ewnglicaꝝ sacerdocij. qm supmi
iuꝛ legē sacdot' filiꝰ pdicart.
Vn et plusqm pphā ē dictꝰ. qui
pmū pphando ueniturū siguit
7 mox uenientē ondendo mon
strauit. Tu· puer pphē sumi sacdos
Qui ei et scdm legē exis
ter posse uidet'. malu
tū docēte intinsecus īcommuta
bili rōne ueritatis noui sacdocij
pco qm ueteris existere successo
7 heres. Maluit decⁿ i spū uo
cari i desertū pplis noui testam
ti sacmēta pdicari. qm ad se
uenientibꝫ i tplm glōso illo te
tpis sacdotij ueteris officiū pee
ptulit lōga solitudīs sitim 7
esuriem. 9tinuus hostiaꝝ sollē
nitas. pilis camelorū et tinctu
zone pellicee aurō textas pōti
ficū ptposuit stolas. Merito
gº sui iusti dicūt parētes. qui
tālem filiū genuerūt. T. cap
Factū ē ūbū dñi ad me
dicens. priusqm te for
mem i utō noui te. 7 anq exi
res d' uentre scificaui te. 7 pphā
i gētibꝫ dedi te. Deo. oratio
Prestā qs ops ds. ut famu
lia tua p uiā salutis in
cedat. ut bi iohnis pcursoris tui
ortamēta sectādo ad eū quē pdix
securā puenīat dnm nrm ihm x' mente
Noli dicē ad iiie. fit. Q
quia puer ego sum qm ad
oīa q̄ mittam te ibis 7 uniūsa que
mādauerō tibi loqris. Do. ad vie
Ecce dedi ūba mā i ore tuo
ecce 9stitui te sup gētes
7 reg̃. ut euellas 7 destruas 7 di
ssipes 7 edifices 7 plātes dic dñs
ops. Do. ad vesperas antiph
Descēdit angls dñi
ad zachariā dicēs
accipe puerū i sen
tute tua et hēbit
nom iohnis baptista p iiii. capl'
Hec dic dns. Audite insule
7 attendite ppli de longe
dns ab utō uocauit me. d' uentre
mris mee rcordatᵘ ē nōis mī. do
R Gabriel anglus appuit zacharie di
cēs nascet' tibi filiꝰ iohnis nomē eꝰ uo
bis. Et multi i natiuite eꝰ gaudebūt V Et
erit magnꝰ corā dnō nā 7 mairꝰ eiꝰ
Ut queant laxis ym. ipē ē. Et
resonare fibris mira gesto
rū famli tuorū solue polluti la
bii reatū scē iohnis Nuncius cel
so ueniēs olympo te pri magn
fore nascituꝝ nom 7 uite seriē
gerēde ordine pmit Ille pmi
ssi dubiꝰ supni pdidit pmte mo

In nomine domini summi et eterni dei nostri ihesu christi. Incipit Pontificale. secundum novum ordinem sancte Romane ecclesie compositum per sanctissimum patrem dominum Johannem papam xxii. Capitulum primum.

Pontifex pueros in fronte chrismare volens paratus cum amictu. Stola. pluviali. albi coloris. et mitra. Premittit admonitionem prout dicetur in titulo de visitandis parochiis. Deinde loto prius et terso pollice dextre manus. Confirmandis genua flectentibus. et iunctis ante pectus manibus. dicit

Spiritus sanctus superveniat in vos et virtus altissimi custodiat vos a peccatis. R. Amen. Deinde dicit. V. Adiutorium nostrum in nomine domini. R. Qui fecit celum et terram. V. Domine exaudi orationem meam. R. Et clamor meus ad te veniat. Dominus vobiscum. R. Et cum spiritu tuo. Oremus. Et tunc elevatis et extensis manibus super confirmandos. dicit hanc orationem.

Omnipotens sempiterne deus qui regenerare dignatus es hos famulos tuos. et famulas tuas. ex aqua et spiritu sancto. Quique dedisti eis remissionem omnium peccatorum. emitte in eos septiformem spiritum tuum paraclitum de celis. R. Amen. Spiritum sapientie et intellectus. R. Amen. Spiritum consilii et fortitudinis. R. Amen. Spiritum scientie et pietatis. R. Amen. Et imple eos spiritu timoris

CLARISSIMI ORATORIS MAGISTRI GEORGII TRAPEZONCII CRETENSIS IN RHETORICOS LIBROS SVOS EXORDIVM

CVM MIHI IN MENTEM VENIAT QVANTA ORATORIAE FACVLTATIS TVM VTILITAS TVM DIGNITAS SIT NON POSSVM NON VEHEMENTER DO

lere q̄d in his nr̄is temporib; nulla fere bonarũ artiũ tam abiecta: atq; contenta habeatur.
[illegible]am etsi non nulle liberaliũ artium ut geometria ut arithmetica et que huius generis
sunt omnino ab usu reciderunt: ne non multũ tam ad hũanitatē ptinere dicā: nō sumus
[illegible] in ipsis tantā passi iacturā quantā in hac humanitatis artiũ pclarissima maxīe
q; necessaria. Nam in illis qdē ita integra subtilissimorũ scriptorũ opa usq; ad p̄ns
extant: ut nihil ei desit qui proficere in eis desideret: nisi studiũ ac diligētia. In
hac ũ dicendi copia q̄nto plures scriptores elegantissimi libri a maiorib; nr̄is tā Lati
nis q̄ grecis relicti sunt: tanto pauciores uel potius nulli his pditis temporib; nr̄is
reperiuntur. Quod siue negligentia oīum siue eorũ q docent: qui q; orationibus
copiā pstitent ignorantia quadā aut pfidia fcm sit: unusqsq; per seipsũ consideret.
[illegible]go id existimo nisi bertolini alani aliorũ q; huiuscemodi libros: nescio an satis utiles
transcribere [illegible] qui docent consta eēt posteritas: aut loco harũ nugarũ: bonorum
auctorũ opa inuenirentur: aut saltē auditores non imbuti his delirationib; nu[illegible]
[illegible]mos ad hũanitatis doctrinas facilius applicaret. qb; nihil unq̄ utilius: nihil dignius
[illegible] pre homi q; deorũ q; tributũ est. Nam philosophia qdē qua omnes liberales ar
[illegible] continent: si dicendi suauitate puata sit: omnē orationē [illegible] infingit atque
con[illegible] totũ q; ingenii sucũ aspitate imbibit nimia. Qd [illegible] mutũ ee sum[illegible]
incomodũ arbitrnt: carere enī oī hũanitate pfecto uidet[illegible] [illegible] pōt: certe et
male loq id uō summo incomodo humanitatis q; [illegible] pximũ ē. Quare posse te
porib; locis psonis causis reb; ornate distincte copiose atq; prudenter [illegible] accomo
[illegible] qd huius artis officiũ est: nō paruę felicitatis existimauerim. Quantus uō ho
[illegible] dignitas in eos qui copiā dicendi adepti sūt confluat: que emolimēta q
cōmoda hoīes eloquētia consequnt: nemo facile poterit explicare. Nam & patriam
[illegible] consiliys sententys q; suis amplificare disertus poterit: et ami[illegible]
psidio et suis ornamento futur[illegible] ē. Preterea inimicis timore: hostib; terrore incuti[illegible]
Q[illegible] macedonũ reges cũ clarissimos oratores ab atheniensib; peteret: ut facilius de[illegible]

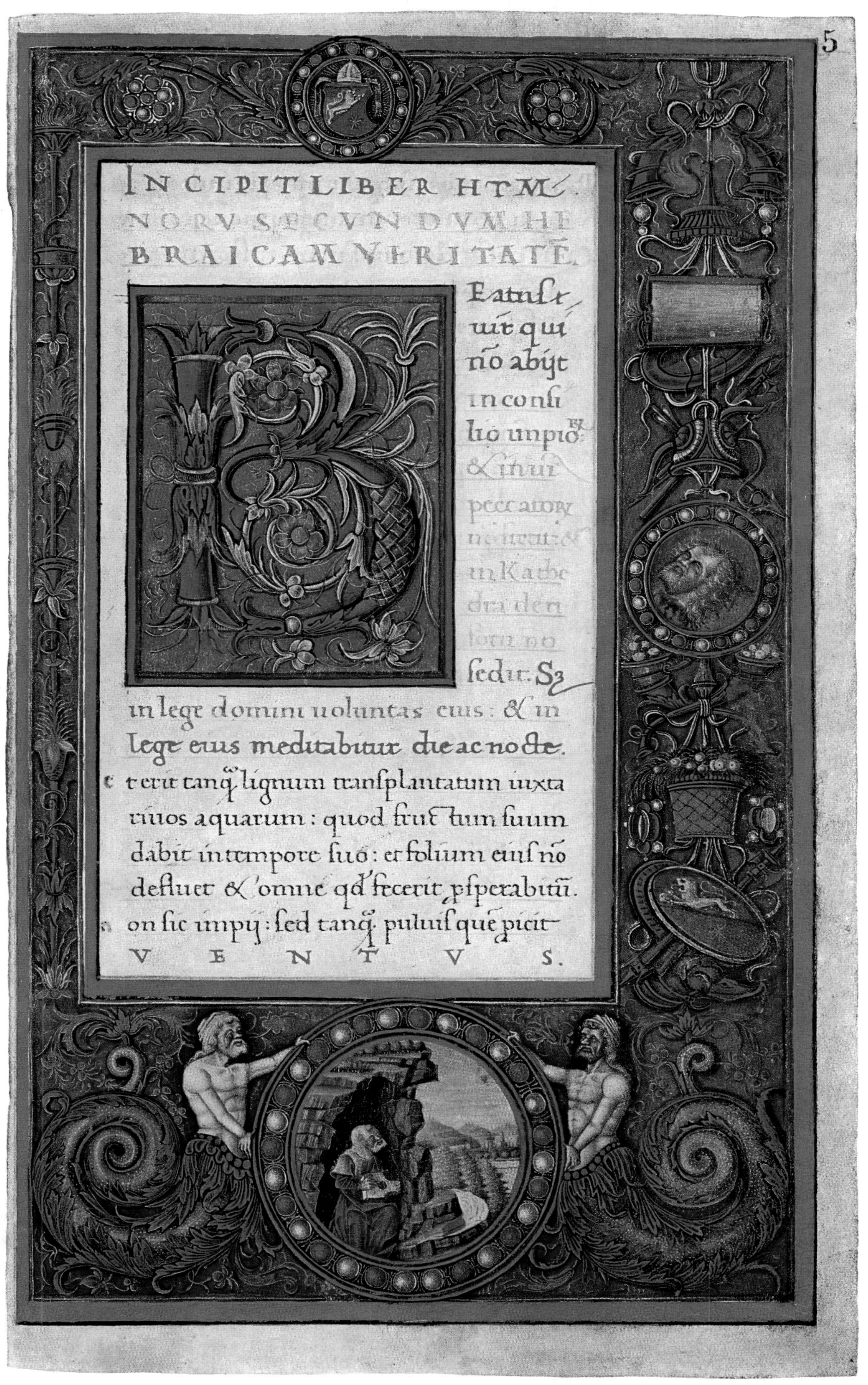

5

INCIPIT LIBER HYM-
NORVM SECVNDVM HE
BRAICAM VERITATE.

Beatus
uir qui
nõ abijt
in consi
lio impio[rum]
& in uia
peccatoru[m]
no[n] stetit: &
in Kathe
dra deri
sorum no[n]
sedit. S[ed]
in lege domini uoluntas eius: & in
lege eius meditabitur die ac nocte.
Et erit tanq[uam] lignum transplantatum iuxta
riuos aquarum: quod fructum suum
dabit in tempore suo: et folium eius no[n]
defluet & omne q[uo]d fecerit p[ro]sperabitur.
Non sic impij: sed tanq[uam] puluis que[m] p[ro]icit
VENTVS.

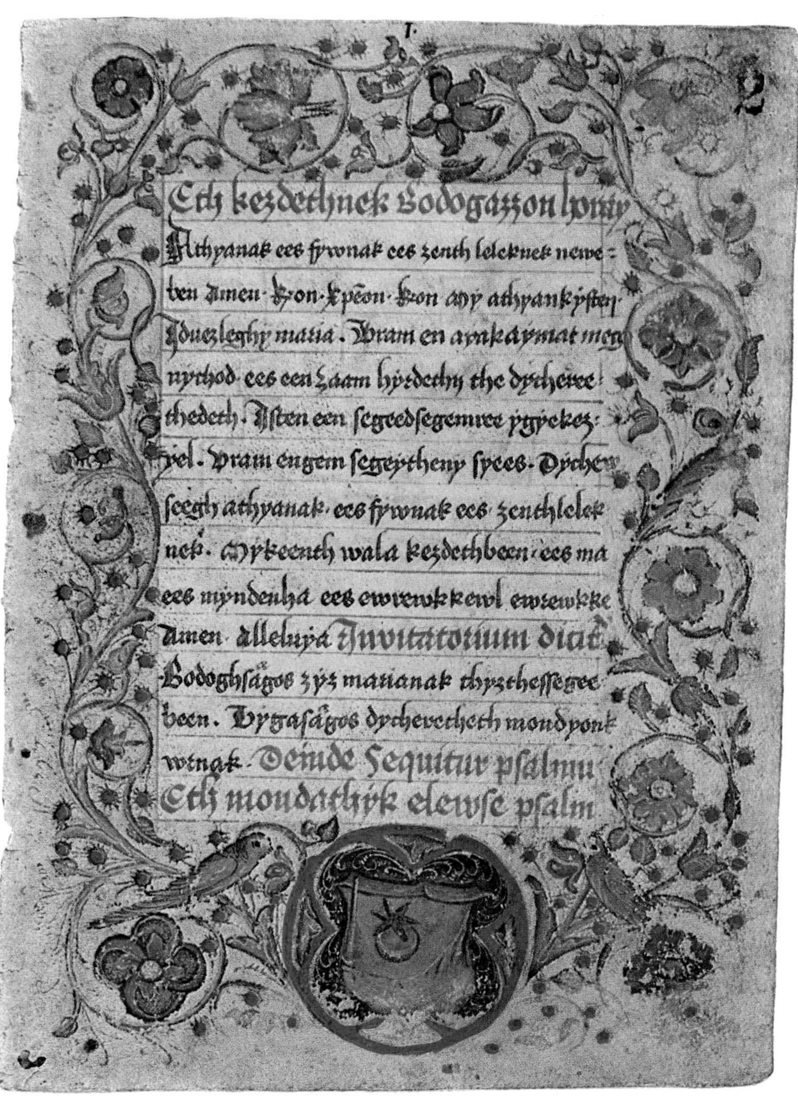
Ezh kezdethnek Bodogazzon hory
Athyanak ees fyvvnak ees zenth leleknek neve-
ben Amen · Kyon · Xpeon · Kyon amy athyank ysten
Idvezlegy maria. Vram en aywkaymat meg
nythod ees een zaam hyrdethy the dycheree
thedeth. Isten een segedsegemree pyryekez
yel. Vram engem segeythenj syees. Dycher
seegh athyanak. ees fyvvnak ees zenthlelek
nek. Mykeenth wala kezdethbeen. ees ma
ees myndenha ees ewrewkkewl ewrewkke
Amen Alleluya Invitatorium dicit
Bodoghsagos zyz marianak thyzthessegee
been. Hyvasagos dycherethet mondyonk
wnyak. Deinde sequitur psalmu
Ezh mondathyk elewse psalm

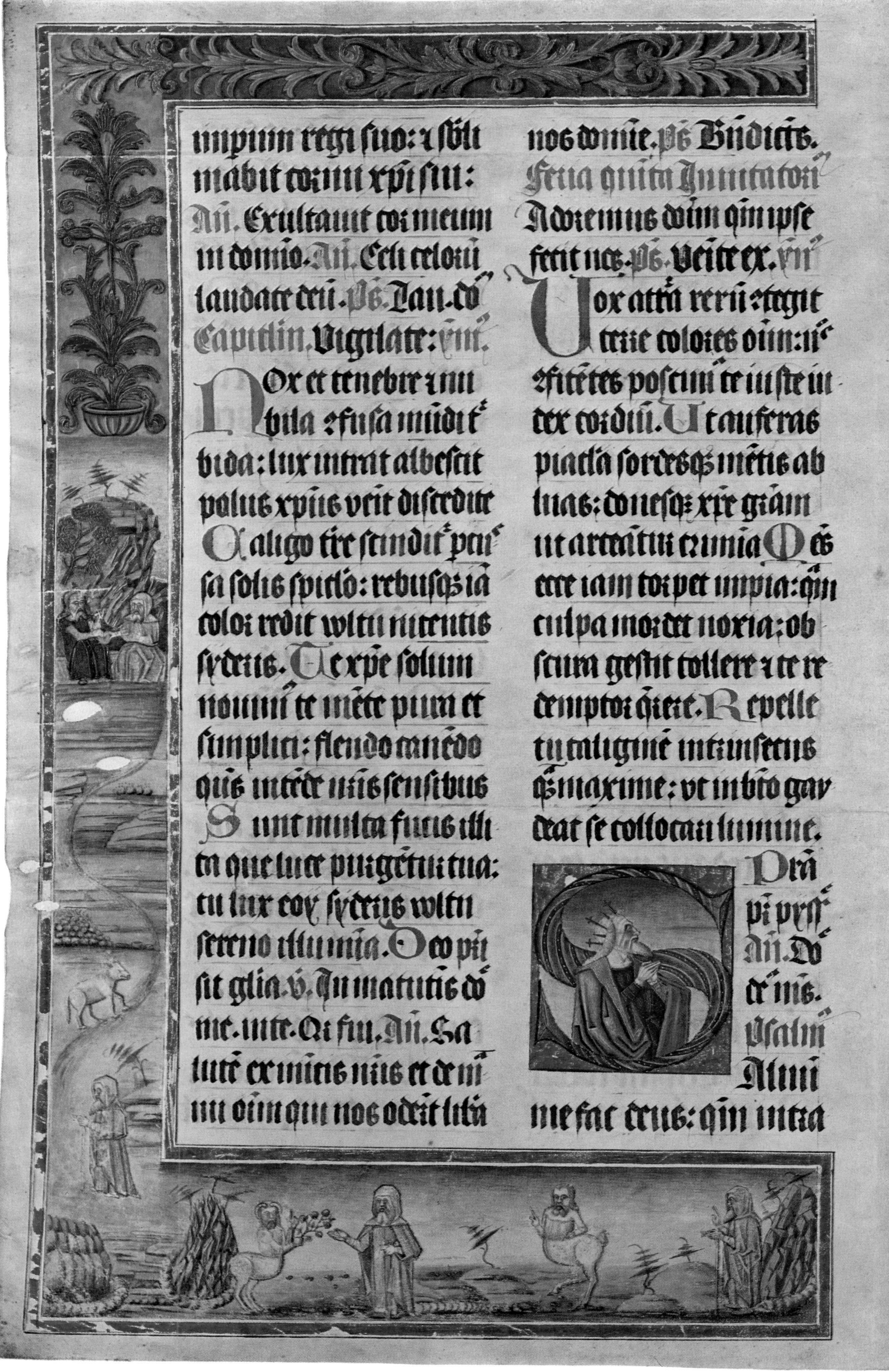

impium regi suo: et sublimabit cornu xpi sui: Aña. Exultavit cor meum in domino. Aña. Celi celorum laudate deum. Ps. Dan. co

Capitulum. Vigilate: ym.

Nox et tenebre et nubila confusa mundi et turbida: lux intrat albescit polus xpus venit discedite. Caligo terre scinditur percussa solis spiculo: rebusque iam color redit vultu nitentis syderis. Te xpe solum novimus te mente pura et simplici: flendo canendo quesumus intende nostris sensibus. Sunt multa fucis illita que luce purgentur tua: tu lux eoi syderis vultu sereno illumina. Deo patri sit gloria. V. In matutinis domine meditabor in te. Qui fui. Aña. Salutem ex inimicis nostris et de manu omnium qui nos oderunt libera nos domine. Ps. Benedictus.

Feria quinta Invitatorium

Adoremus dominum quoniam ipse fecit nos. Ps. Venite ex. ym.

Nox atra rerum contegit terre colores omnium: nos confitentes poscimus te iuste iudex cordium. Ut auferas piacula sordesque mentis abluas: donesque xpe gratiam ut arceantur crimina. Mens ecce torpet impia: quam culpa mordet noxia: obscura gestit tollere et te redemptor querere. Repelle tu caliginem intrinsecus quam maxime: ut in beato gaudeat se collocari lumine.

[illegible] Aña. Do[illegible]

Psalm

alvum me fac deus: quoniam intra

In gallicantu. Sequentia sancti Evangelii: Secundum Lucam. In illo tempore:
Exiit edictum a cesare augusto: ut describeretur universus orbis. Hec descriptio prima: facta est a preside Syrie Cyrino. Et ibant omnes. ut profiterentur: singuli in suam civitatem. Ascendit autem et Joseph a galilea de civitate nazareth: in iudeam civitatem david. que vocatur bethlehem. eo quod esset de domo

XXXVIII

te levavi
animam me
am deus meus in te con
fido non erubescam neq;
irrideant me inimici mei

cōmouebitur para ta se des tu a
de us extunc a seculo tu es
xulta fi li a sy on lauda filia cō
iherusalem ecce rex tuus ve nit san
Missa sūma.
ctus et saluatō mūdi
uer natus est nobis
et fi lius datus est nobis cuius im

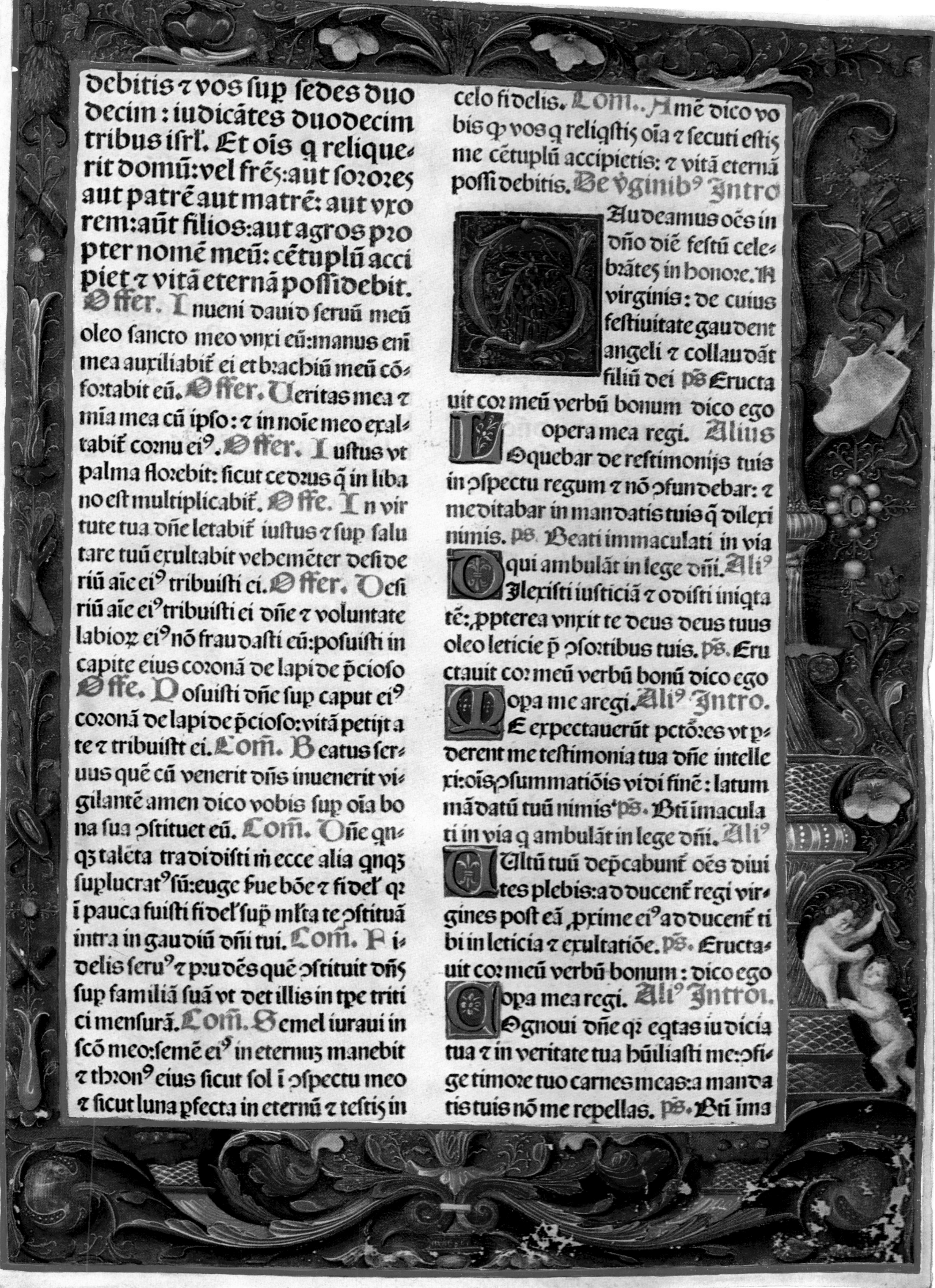

debitis ⁊ vos sup sedes duo
decim: iudicātes duodecim
tribus isrl'. Et oīs q̄ relique-
rit domū: vel frēs: aut sorores
aut patrē aut matrē: aut vxo
rem: aūt filios: aut agros pro
pter nomē meū: cētuplū acci
piet ⁊ vitā eternā possidebit.
Offer. Inueni dauid seruū meū
oleo sancto meo vnxi eū: manus eni
mea auxiliabit' ei et brachiū meū cō-
fortabit eū. Offer. Ueritas mea ⁊
mīa mea cū ipso: ⁊ in noīe meo exal-
tabit' cornu eiꝰ. Offer. Iustus vt
palma florebit: sicut cedrus q̄ in liba
no est multiplicabit'. Offe. In vir
tute tua dn̄e letabit' iustus ⁊ sup salu
tare tuū exultabit vehemēter desi de
riū aīe eiꝰ tribuisti ei. Offer. Desi
riū aīe eiꝰ tribuisti ei dn̄e ⁊ voluntate
labioꝝ eiꝰ nō fraudasti eū: posuisti in
capite eius coronā de lapide p̄cioso
Offe. Posuisti dn̄e sup caput eiꝰ
coronā de lapide p̄cioso: vitā petijt a
te ⁊ tribuistt ei. Cōm. Beatus ser-
uus quē cū venerit dn̄s inuenerit vi-
gilantē amen dico vobis sup oīa bo
na sua ꝯstituet eū. Cōm. Dn̄e qn-
q̄ talēta tradidisti m̄ ecce alia qnq̄
suplucratꝰ sū: euge ꝗue bōe ⁊ fidel' q̄
i pauca fuisti fidel' sup̄ mlta te ꝯstituā
intra in gaudiū dn̄i tui. Cōm. Fidelis seruꝰ ⁊ prudēs quē ꝯstituit dn̄s
sup familiā suā vt det illis in tpe triti
ci mensurā. Cōm. Semel iuraui in
scō meo: semē eiꝰ in eternuʒ manebit
⁊ thronꝰ eius sicut sol i ꝯspectu meo
⁊ sicut luna pfecta in eternū ⁊ testis in

celo fidelis. Cōm. Amē dico vo
bis q̄ vos q̄ reliqstis oīa ⁊ secuti estis
me cētuplū accipietis: ⁊ vitā eternā
possidebitis. De v̄ginibꝰ Intro
Gaudeamus oēs in
dn̄o diē festū cele-
brātes in honore. B.
virginis: de cuius
festiuitate gaudent
angeli ⁊ collaudāt
filiū dei ps Eructa
uit cor meū verbū bonum dico ego
opera mea regi. Alius
Loquebar de testimonijs tuis
in ꝯspectu regum ⁊ nō ꝯfundebar: ⁊
meditabar in mandatis tuis q̄ dilexi
nimis. ps. Beati immaculati in via
qui ambulāt in lege dn̄i. Aliꝰ
Dilexisti iusticiā ⁊ odisti iniqta
tē: ꝓpterea vnxit te deus deus tuus
oleo leticie p̄ ꝯsortibus tuis. ps. Eru
ctauit cor meū verbū bonū dico ego
opa me aregi. Aliꝰ Intro.
Me expectauerūt pctōres vt p-
derent me testimonia tua dn̄e intelle
xi: oīs ꝯsummatiōis vidi finē: latum
mādatū tuū nimis. ps. Btī imacula
ti in via q̄ ambulāt in lege dn̄i. Aliꝰ
Uultū tuū dep̄cabunt' oēs diui
tes plebis: adducent' regi vir-
gines post eā ꝓxime eiꝰ adducent' ti
bi in leticia ⁊ exultatiōe. ps. Eructa-
uit cor meū verbū bonum: dico ego
opa mea regi. Aliꝰ Introi.
Cognoui dn̄e q̄ eqtas iudicia
tua ⁊ in veritate tua hūiliasti me: ꝯfi-
ge timore tuo carnes meas: a manda
tis tuis nō me repellas. ps. Btī ima

XLIII

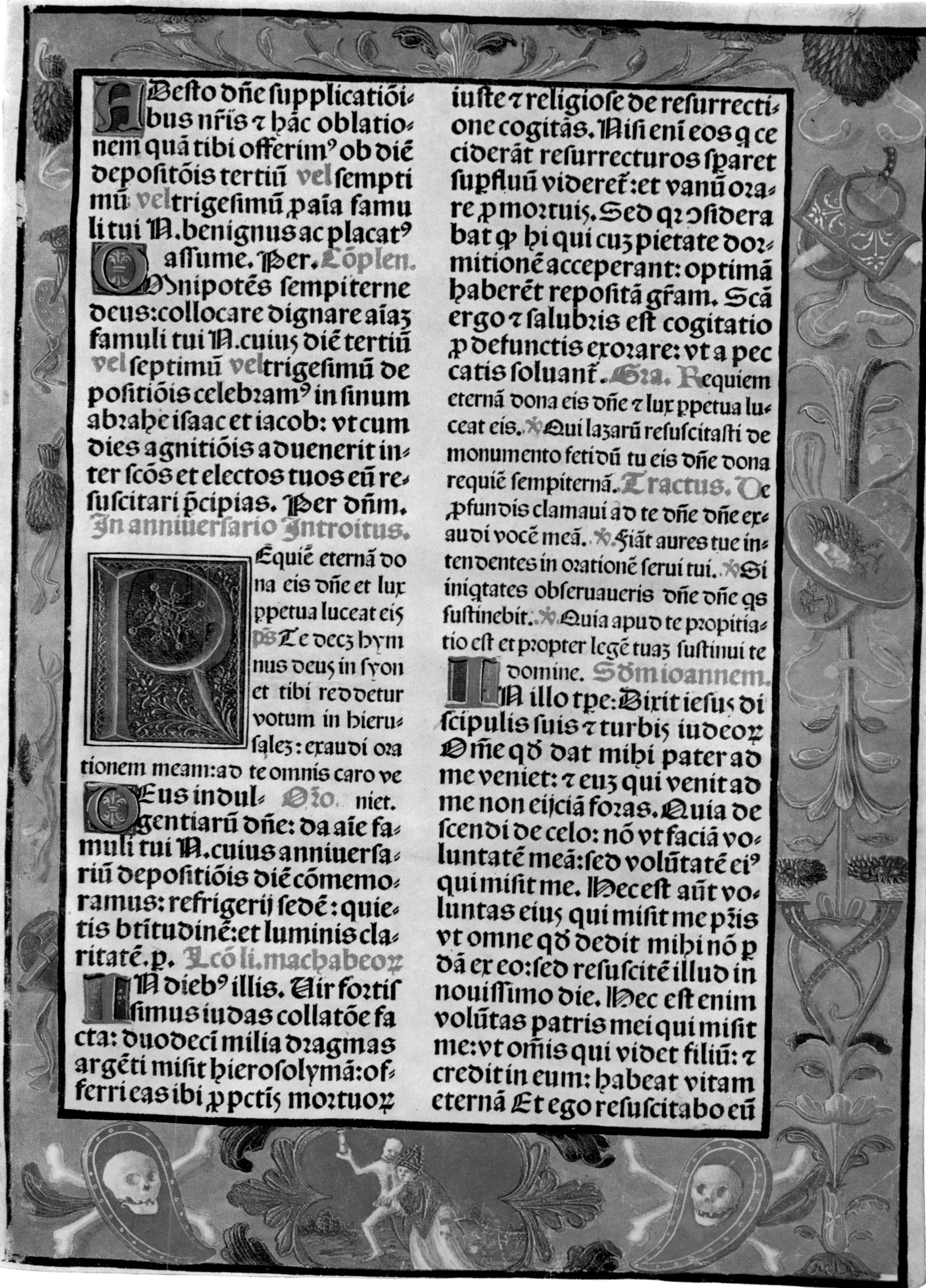

Adesto dñe supplicatiōi-
bus nr̄is ꝛ hāc oblatio-
nem quā tibi offerim⁹ ob diē
depositōis tertiū vel sempti
mū: vel trigesimū ꝑ aīa famu
li tui N. benignus ac placat⁹
assume. Per. Cōplen.

Omnipotēs sempiterne
deus: collocare dignare aīaꝫ
famuli tui N. cuius diē tertiū
vel septimū vel trigesimū de
positiōis celebram⁹ in sinum
abrahe isaac et iacob: vt cum
dies agnitiōis aduenerit inter scōs et electos tuos eū re-
suscitari ꝑcipias. Per dñm.

In anniuersario Introitus.

Requiē eternā do
na eis dñe et lux
ꝑpetua luceat eis
ps. Te decꝫ hym
nus deus in syon
et tibi reddetur
votum in hieru-
salez: exaudi ora
tionem meam: ad te omnis caro ve
niet. Orō.

Deus indul-
gentiarū dñe: da aīe fa-
muli tui N. cuius anniuersa-
riū depositiōis diē cōmemo-
ramus: refrigerij sedē: quie-
tis btitudinē: et luminis cla-
ritatē. p. Lcō li. machabeoꝝ

In dieb⁹ illis. Uir fortis
simus iudas collatōe fa
cta: duodeci milia dragmas
argēti misit hierosolymā: of-
ferri eas ibi ꝑ pctis mortuoꝝ
iuste ꝛ religiose de resurrecti-
one cogitās. Nisi enī eos q̄ ce
ciderāt resurrecturos sparet
supfluū videret: et vanū ora-
re ꝑ mortuis. Sed q̄r ɔsidera
bat q̄ hi qui cuꝫ pietate dor-
mitionē acceperant: optimā
haberēt repositā grām. Scā
ergo ꝛ salubris est cogitatio
ꝑ defunctis exorare: vt a pec
catis soluant̄. Grā. Requiem
eternā dona eis dñe ꝛ lux ꝑpetua luceat eis. ℣. Qui lazarū resuscitasti de
monumento fetidū tu eis dñe dona
requiē sempiternā. Tractus. De
ꝑfundis clamaui ad te dñe dñe exaudi vocē meā. ℣. Fiāt aures tue in-
tendentes in oratione serui tui. ℣. Si
iniqtates obseruaueris dñe dñe qs
sustinebit. ℣. Quia apud te propitia-
tio est et propter legē tuaꝫ sustinui te
domine. Sc̄dm ioannem.

In illo tpe: Dixit iesus di
scipulis suis ꝛ turbis iudeoꝝ
Omē qd dat mihi pater ad
me veniet: ꝛ euꝫ qui venit ad
me non eijciā foras. Quia de
scendi de celo: nō vt faciā vo-
luntatē meā: sed volūtatē ei⁹
qui misit me. Hec est aūt vo-
luntas eius qui misit me p̄ris
vt omne qd dedit mihi nō ꝑ
dā ex eo: sed resuscitē illud in
nouissimo die. Hec est enim
volūtas patris mei qui misit
me: vt oīs qui videt filiū: ꝛ
credit in eum: habeat vitam
eternā Et ego resuscitabo eū